MW00856645

The Practitioner's Guide to Program Management

Irene Didinsky, MBA, PMP

Library of Congress Cataloging-in-Publication Data

Names: Didinsky, Irene, author.
Title: Practitioners' guide to program management / Irene Didinsky, MBA, PMP.
Description: Newtown Square, PA : Project Management Institute, [2017] |
   Includes bibliographical references.
Identifiers: LCCN 2017013189| ISBN 9781628253689 (paper back : alk. paper) |
   ISBN 9781628253696 (epub) | ISBN 9781628253702 (kindle) | ISBN
   9781628253719 (web pdf)
Subjects: LCSH: Project management. | Strategic planning. | Organizational change.

Classification: LCC HD69.P75 .D533 2017 | DDC 658.4/04--dc23 LC record available at https://lccn.loc.gov/2017013189

ISBN: 978-1-62825-368-9

Published by: Project Management Institute, Inc.
            14 Campus Boulevard
            Newtown Square, Pennsylvania 19073-3299 USA
            Phone: +610-356-4600
            Fax: +610-356-4647
            Email: customercare@pmi.org
            Internet: PMI.org

©2017 Project Management Institute, Inc. All rights reserved.

"PMI", the PMI logo, "PMP", the PMP logo, "PMBOK", "PgMP", "Project Management Journal", "PM Network", and the PMI Today logo are registered marks of Project Management Institute, Inc. The Quarter Globe Design is a trademark of the Project Management Institute, Inc. For a comprehensive list of PMI marks, contact the PMI Legal Department.

PMI Publications welcomes corrections and comments on its books. Please feel free to send comments on typographical, formatting, or other errors. Simply make a copy of the relevant page of the book, mark the error, and send it to: Book Editor, PMI Publications, 14 Campus Boulevard, Newtown Square, PA 19073-3299 USA.

To inquire about discounts for resale or educational purposes, please contact the PMI Book Service Center.

            PMI Book Service Center
            P.O. Box 932683, Atlanta, GA 31193-2683 USA
            Phone: 1-866-276-4764 (within the U.S. or Canada) or +1-770-280-4129 (globally)
            Fax: +1-770-280-4113
            Email: info@bookorders.pmi.org

Printed in the United States of America. No part of this work may be reproduced or transmitted in any form or by any means, electronic, manual, photocopying, recording, or by any information storage and retrieval system, without prior written permission of the publisher.

The paper used in this book complies with the Permanent Paper Standard issued by the National Information Standards Organization (Z39.48—1984).

10 9 8 7 6 5

To my beloved sons Arthur and Samuel.

Contents

Executive Summary

There are many factors that may contribute to a failure in program execution: knowledge gap around program management, variations in definition across organizations and industries, and lack of a standardized approach. There are very few books published and very few training opportunities offered on the topic of program management.

The Practitioner's Guide to Program Management closes the knowledge gap around program management and offers a first-of-its-kind program management desktop manual. The purpose of the book is to define program management and outline an approach to it, illustrated with real-life examples. To date, this critical approach has not been well-defined and documented, and has frequently been left to the knowledge and expertise of program managers engaged in actual work.

Why do organizations undertake programs and projects? What is a program, and how is it different from a project? How to implement a program? This book will provide answers to these and many other questions.

Author Irene Didinsky walks the readers through all key components of program management, discussing what makes a successful program manager, the importance of a program alignment with the organizational strategy, how a program realizes benefits, program management infrastructure, and much more. This systematic approach to program management will guarantee successful program execution. It will also help standardize a program management approach and reduce the number of variations that currently exist. Each chapter of the book includes practical examples.

The book is a one-of-a-kind academic practitioner's guide, with each page containing substantial potential benefits to the readers. The book's structure and language are easy to follow. It is illustrated with helpful graphical images that illustrate key terms and concepts.

What Is Program Management? The first chapter constructs a time line that depicts key milestones in the evolution of the program and project management industries. It analyzes the current state of the program management industry, identifying gaps, the closure of which will ensure future industry growth. It defines what a program is and compares it to a project and a portfolio, illustrating roles that each plays in executing organizational strategy. The chapter also delineates why organizations deploy and execute programs.

What Makes a Successful Program Manager? A program manager is a key driver of a successful program execution. A program manager executes a program by setting up program structure, leading project managers, and delivering program benefits. That is why it is very important to define the program manager role and understand what helps a program manager succeed.

The second chapter describes how the organizational structure defines a program manager role. The chapter introduces the program management continuum, a concept that defines four phases within the project-oriented and program-oriented organizational structures. It defines the program manager role in each phase of the program management continuum. The chapter illustrates how program infrastructure enables a program manager to lead. It also introduces a proficiency framework, examining proficiencies that make a successful program manager. The chapter concludes with a table that compares program, project, and portfolio managers' roles.

Program Strategy Alignment: This chapter provides an in-depth analysis of the program strategy alignment domain. The chapter describes the criticality of program alignment with the organizational strategy. It describes elements that a program manager and a program sponsor create to ensure program strategy alignment throughout the program life cycle. These elements include the program business case, road map, environmental analysis, and phase-gate review.

During the definition phase, to ensure program initial alignment with the organizational strategy, a program manager creates a business case and a road map. The program manager conducts an environmental analysis, the results of which become an input to the business case and a road map. During the benefits delivery phase, a program manager conducts phase-gate reviews to ensure the program's continued alignment with the organizational strategy.

Program Benefits Realization and Management: Benefits realization is one of the main reasons organizations employ programs. This chapter provides an in-depth analysis of the program benefits realization domain. It defines a benefit and describes various types of benefits that programs realize. And it defines a business value and business results, helping us understand the differences between the two and providing examples of each. Analyzing the program management continuum, it shows how benefits delivery increases as the organization moves from the project-oriented to the program-oriented structure. The chapter also describes that benefits management is achieved by employing the benefits management strategy that includes five phases: benefits identification, benefits analysis and planning, benefits delivery, benefits transition, and benefits sustainment.

Stakeholder Engagement: As stakeholders have a different level of interest in the program, it is important to manage their expectations based on their needs. The chapter describes the stakeholder engagement domain, including how to engage and manage stakeholders. It introduces a stakeholder map, a tool that allows managing stakeholders. The chapter concludes by describing how to manage conflicting priorities of stakeholders.

Program Governance and Team Management: Using the program management continuum, the chapter defines the program governance domain. It illustrates how the organizational structure defines the program governance structure. The chapter defines program governance roles and shows how each role fits within the program governance structure. It also examines how these roles work together as a program team. The chapter defines three main functional areas within a program team, showing what roles are included in each functional area and responsibilities that each functional area performs. The chapter concludes by describing how a program manager builds, leads, and off-boards a program team.

Program Life Cycle Management: This chapter defines the program life cycle domain and outlines a detailed approach to program execution through the program life cycle. A program delivers benefits by executing a set of phases, which constitute a program life cycle. A program life cycle includes three phases: definition, benefits delivery, and closure. A purpose of the definition phase is to expand the business case and strategic plan objectives, and fully define expected program outcomes. A purpose of the benefits delivery phase is to integrate and manage program components to facilitate the delivery of the intended program benefits. A purpose of the closure phase is to execute a controlled closure of the program.

Program Management Infrastructure: This chapter starts by describing how a program manager uses procurement in the delivery of program benefits. It examines program infrastructure, including systems and tools needed to manage a program effectively. The chapter describes how to build and maintain a program management plan, a key document that ensures program alignment with the organizational strategy, and benefits delivery, on budget and on time. The chapter analyzes tools for program monitoring and periodic evaluation. This chapter also defines risks and examines risk management and escalation mechanisms. It concludes by describing program change process, quality control process, and program communication. This chapter can be used as a desktop manual, as it includes multiple program management tools and templates.

Effective Program Management: A program manager monitors program execution during the entire program life cycle and ensures program benefits delivery on time and on budget as well as ensures effective resource management. This chapter describes, in detail, activities and tools that can be used to deliver a program on time. It also describes program financial management that is necessary to deliver it on a budget, including budget, forecast, and actual costs management during each phase of the program. Each calculation is illustrated with examples of the financial management tables and accompanied with detailed descriptions on how to construct them. The chapter concludes with the effective resource management during each phase of the program, including resource forecasting, estimation, and actual tracking.

Future of Program Management: This chapter discusses the future of the program management industry. To understand how the industry can grow and where it can improve, the chapter examines the current state of the program management industry, focusing on existing gaps. As the program management industry operates globally, the chapter discusses the global environment and future trends. Using the program management industry's current state and global environment future trends, the chapter attempts to define the future state of the program management industry.

Program Managers Community of Practice (PgMCoP): A program manager needs to understand the organizational environment as it defines the program management structure and sculpts the program manager role. A program manager should influence the business-focused program management structure as it empowers a business-focused program manager role. One of the venues that a program manager can utilize is the program management community of practice (PgMCoP). A community of practice can serve as a forum for program management current state analysis, program process improvement initiative discussions, and program best practices and knowledge sharing. This chapter defines the community of practice value to organizations and program managers, and describes their foundation, structure, and operations.

This book serves as a much-needed practitioner's guide to program management. It also provides a foundation for program management training classes. Above all, it contributes to program management industry standardization.

CHAPTER 1

What Is Program Management?

The chapter constructs a time line that depicts key milestones in the evolution of the program and project management industries. It analyzes the program management industry's current state, identifying gaps, the closure of which will ensure future industry growth. It defines a program and compares it to a project and a portfolio, illustrating roles that each play in executing organizational strategy. The chapter also delineates why organizations deploy programs and how organizations execute them.

The chapter includes the following sections:

- Program management industry history and current state;
- Program, project, and portfolio definitions;
- Why organizations deploy programs;
- Program management performance domains; and
- Program life cycle management.

Program Management Industry History and Current State

To ensure the organization is successfully and effectively employing program management, it is important to understand the history of the program management industry as well as its current state. The program management industry is affected by the project management industry in many ways. So, to understand how the program management industry evolved, we will construct a time line that shows key milestones in the evolution of the program and project management industries.

We will also analyze the current state of the program management industry and identify gaps, the closure of which will ensure future industry growth.

Program management evolved in the 1940s in the United States military. The Manhattan Project, which created the atomic bomb, first used program management concepts. However, it was not until the 1980s when some commercial companies started to adopt program management concepts and tools in their operations.

Project management evolved at around same time as program management. In the 1950s, organizations started to apply formalized project management approaches, tools, and techniques. However, for thousands of years, dating as far back as to the time of the construction of the Egyptian pyramids and the Great Wall of China, mankind practiced forms of project management.

The time line in Figure 1-1 depicts key milestones in the evolution of the program and project management industries:

1940

1. In the 1940s, the Manhattan Project, which created the atomic bomb, first introduced program management concepts.

1950

2. In the 1950s, the Atlas project that created the first U.S. intercontinental ballistic missile, used program management practices.
3. Project management practice in the modern sense began in the 1950s. Even though in some form, project management concepts were used in early civilizations.

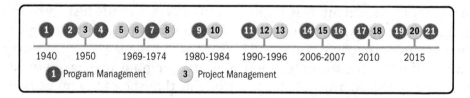

Figure 1-1: Key milestones in the evolution of the program and project management industries.

4. Program management's first documented evidence dates back to 1957, when the U.S. Department of the Navy formed the first program office, called the Special Project Office (SPO).

1969

5. Project Management Institute (PMI) was founded in 1969.

1971

6. The first program management course was conducted by The College of Defence Management in 1971.

1974

7. The first PMI chapter was chartered in Houston, Texas in 1974.

1980

8. Program management practice started to expand into public and private organizations in many industries.
9. The manufacturing and software development sectors used project management practices.

1984

10. In 1984, PMI instituted the Project Management Professional (PMP)® certification.

1990

11. Program management practice continued to expand, and organizations began defining program management and started developing homegrown methodologies for program execution. Definitions and methodologies were not standardized and varied significantly among different organizations.
12. Different industries and organizations widely used project management theories, tools, and techniques.

1996

13. PMI first published *A Guide to the Project Management Body of Knowledge (PMBOK® Guide)* in 1996. The guide provided the project management industry with standardized definitions and methodologies.

2006

14. PMI first published *The Standard for Program Management* in 2006. To date, PMI published two subsequent editions. The standard provided the program management industry with standardized definitions and methodologies.
15. *Pulse of the Profession®*, the project management industry annual report, was first published by PMI in 2006. The program management industry does not have an industry report. However, the project management industry reports frequently include program management industry data.

2007

16. In 2007, PMI instituted the Program Management Professional (PgMP)® certification.

2010

17. The program management industry continued to grow and reported that, in 2010, 62% and in 2011, 65% of organizations always or often used program management.[1]
18. The project management industry continued to grow and reported that, in 2010, 59% and in 2011, 63% of organizations used standardized project management across all departments.[2]

---

[1] PMI. (2012). *Pulse of the profession®: Driving success in challenging times.* Newtown Square, PA: Author.

[2] PMI. (2012). *Pulse of the profession®: Driving success in challenging times.* Newtown Square, PA: Author.

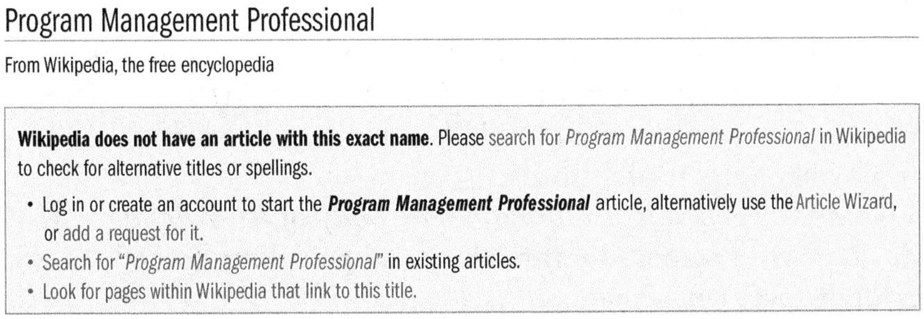

Program Management Professional

From Wikipedia, the free encyclopedia

Wikipedia does not have an article with this exact name. Please search for *Program Management Professional* in Wikipedia to check for alternative titles or spellings.

- Log in or create an account to start the ***Program Management Professional*** article, alternatively use the Article Wizard, or add a request for it.
- Search for "*Program Management Professional*" in existing articles.
- Look for pages within Wikipedia that link to this title.

Figure 1-2: Wikipedia, the free encyclopedia, does not have a page for the Program Management Professional (PgMP)® certification.

19. Program Management Professional (PgMP)® certification holders included 1,200 persons, as reported by PMI in February 2015.[3]

2015

20. Project Management Professional (PMP)® certification holders included 647,663 persons, as reported by PMI in February 2015.[4]
21. The Program Management Professional (PgMP)® certification did not have a page in Wikipedia, the Free Encyclopedia, in December 2015, as shown in Figure 1-2. The Project Management Professional (PMP)® certification does have a page in Wikipedia.

The key milestones in the evolution of the program and project management industries time line contained a few terms that are defined as follows:

The Project Management Institute (PMI) is an international organization advancing the professional field of project management. It does this by setting standards, through certified education and development, and by conducting research and professional conferencing.

---

[3] PMI. (2015). *PMI-Certification-Overview-Kronos.pptx*. Newtown Square, PA: Author.

[4] PMI. (2015). *PMI-Certification-Overview-Kronos.pptx*. Newtown Square, PA: Author.

The Project Management Professional (PMP)® is the most important industry-recognized certification for project managers.[5]

The Program Management Professional (PgMP)® is a visible sign of your advanced experience and skill and gives you a distinct advantage in employment and promotion.[6]

A Guide to the Project Management Body of Knowledge (PMBOK® Guide) is a set of standard terminology and guidelines (a body of knowledge) for project management.

The Standard for Program Management is the first document that provided a detailed understanding of program management, defined a standardized approach to it, and outlined methodologies to execute programs.

Even though the program and project management industries evolved at about same time and have grown since their inception, the program management industry has grown at a slower pace than the project management industry. As a result, a lot of research has gone into the project management industry and not into the program management industry.

A program management industry expert stated that he has not seen so much research for trends in the program management industry. Also, even in the research for project management, he has noted that there is confusion between the management of a project and program, due to unclear and inconsistent definitions used by many organizations.[7]

We will analyze the current state of the program management industry by comparing it to the current state of the project management industry in the key areas of industry growth, strategy alignment, and standardization.

Program Management Industry Growth

Program management practice exists in the United States; however, it is not widespread. Project management practice is common in the United States, and is widespread. Program management has some

---

[5] http:// http://www.pmi.org/certifications/types/project-management-pmp

[6] http:// http://www.pmi.org/certifications/types/program-management-pgmp

[7] Interview with Sankaran Ramani, MoP, MSP, P3O, CM, PMP, PgMP, PfMP, Director, GRT Consulting LLP

global recognition, while project management has wide global recognition. The number of facts confirms limited growth and spread of the program management industry.

In 2010, almost 5.5 million jobs in the United States were in project management. By 2020, that figure is expected to increase to almost 6.2 million, or a double-digit growth of more than 12%. Project management is practiced globally. Between 2010 and 2020, the project management profession is slated to grow globally by US$6.61 trillion.[8]

Program management industry analysis is rather limited; that is why similar data on industry domestic and international current size and future growth are not available. Available data can confirm larger growth in the project management industry compared to the program management industry. For example, 41% of organizations are extremely or very focused on the training and development of employees in project management, while only 18% of organizations are focused on the training and development of employees in program management. Highly developed organizational cultures of agility focus significantly more on the training and development of employees compared with underdeveloped organizational cultures:

- Project management: 66% versus 13% of underdeveloped cultures; and
- Program management: 44% versus 4% of underdeveloped cultures.[9]

Agility refers to an iterative, incremental method of managing the design and build activities of engineering, information technology, and other business areas that aim to provide new product or service development in a highly flexible and interactive manner.[10]

---

[8] PMI. (2013). *PMI's industry growth forecast: Project management between 2010 + 2020.* Retrieved from http://www.pmi.org/-/media/pmi/documents/public/pdf/business-solutions/project-management-skills-gap-report.pdf

[9] PMI. (2015). *Pulse of the profession®: Capturing the value of project management through organizational agility.* Newtown Square, PA: Author.

[10] Agile management. (n.d.). In *Wikipedia.* Retrieved from https://en.wikipedia.org/wiki/Agile_management

More organizations use project management, where 31% always use it, 35% often use it, 22% sometimes use it, 9% rarely use it, and 3% never use it. Fewer organizations use program management, where only 27% always use it, 33% often use it, 24% sometimes use it, 10% rarely use it, and 10% never use it.[11] In the study conducted by PMI in late 2011, just over 40% of respondents indicated having project manager roles, while significantly fewer respondents, or only 15%, indicated having program manager roles.[12]

The data presented above confirm that the program management industry experienced slower growth than the project management industry did. This conclusion is further confirmed by the scarce availability of program management industry data, and confusion between project and program management industry data due to unclear definitions.

Program Strategy Alignment

Organizations deploy programs and projects to execute organizational strategy and implement change. "I do not differentiate strategy implementation and project success," said Daniel Svoboda, PMP, Program Manager, Key Bank. "Every project that a company does should align with the strategy in some way."[13]

And yet, only a limited number of organizations report program and project alignment with the organizational strategy. Limited data are available on project alignment with organizational strategy. Only 43% of organizations report high alignment of projects with the organizational strategy. Out of the remaining organizations, 47% report medium, and 11% report low alignment of projects with the organizational strategy.[14] No data could be found on program alignment with the organizational strategy. So, we assume that less than a half of organizations achieve high alignment of programs with the organizational strategy.

---

[11] PMI. (2015). *Pulse of the profession®: Capturing the value of project management.* Newtown Square, PA: Author.

[12] PMI. (2012). *Pulse of the profession®: Driving success in challenging times.* Newtown Square, PA: Author.

[13] (PMI). (2015). *Pulse of the profession®: Capturing the value of project management.* Newtown Square, PA: Author.

[14] PMI. (2015). *Pulse of the profession®: Capturing the value of project management.* Newtown Square, PA: Author.

Program Management Industry Standardization

To date, the program management industry has not achieved the same level of standardization as the project management industry has. As a result, program management industry definitions, methodologies, and tools vary significantly among organizations and industries. Organizations frequently develop program management definitions. And, as there are mostly project management methodologies and tools available, organizations either develop homegrown program management methodologies and tools or adopt them from the project management industry. This further contributes to the significant variations in program management industry definitions, methodologies, and tools.

PMI is one of the key institutions that sets and promotes standardization in the program management and project management industries. To date, the project management industry has benefited from a larger standardization effort, as it grew faster and with greater magnitude than the program management industry. For example, PMI published *The Standard for Program Management* in 2006, 19 years later than it published *A Guide to the Project Management Body of Knowledge (PMBOK® Guide)*.

The PgMP certification was instituted in 2007, 23 years later than the PMP certification was instituted. In the eight years since its institution, the PgMP certification has not achieved growth comparable with PMP certification growth. As of February 2015, PMI reported only 1,200 certified PgMPs, a very small number compared to the 647,663 certified PMPs. A significant discrepancy in the number of PgMP-certified professionals compared to the number of PMP-certified professionals, confirms that only a small number of program managers are well-familiar with the program management industry standards.

PMI instituted PMI local chapters in 1974, providing a forum for project management practitioners. As of January 2016, PMI members did not have local chapters for program management practitioners or for any other certification, identifying a need for a program management community of practice (PgMCoP). The community of practice can serve as an important step in growing the program management industry and as a critical step in achieving standardization around program management definitions, methodologies, and tools. Chapter 11 of this book defines the program management community of practice (PgMCoP) as a forum that allows program managers to share ideas, knowledge, best practices, program execution mechanisms, and tools. The chapter describes the value of the community of practice to program managers and organizations as well as explains how to found, structure, and operate a PgMCoP.

PMI currently publishes the *Project Management Journal®* (PMJ), which sometimes includes articles on program management. However, as of December 2016, PMI did not have a program management industry journal. Since 2006, PMI has been publishing the *Pulse of the Profession®*, its annual project management industry survey that sometimes includes program management industry data. However, as of January 2016, PMI has not had a program management industry annual survey. As the program management industry continues to grow, it is important to improve industry standardization around definitions, methodologies, and tools.

Program, Project, and Portfolio Definitions

Many organizations still struggle to distinguish program management from project management, and research confirms that program management definitions vary significantly among companies and industries. Often, program management is defined as the management of multiple projects that have common funding and stakeholders. As program management definitions vary, so do program management approaches, methodologies, and tools.

A *program* is a group of related projects, subprojects, and program operational management activities, managed in a coordinated way to obtain benefits not available from managing them individually.[15] Among numerous examples of programs, is a program to develop a new product, to implement a process improvement effort, to modernize business, and to ensure regulatory compliance.

Programs include individual projects and subprograms. A *subprogram* is a program that includes individual projects and is managed as a part of another program. Programs also include elements of related work outside the scope of the discrete projects in the program, called *program operational management*. Any part of the program described earlier, including subprogram, projects, and program operational management activities, can be referred to as a program *component*.

---

[15] PMI. (2013). *The standard for program management* – Third edition. Newtown Square, PA: Author.

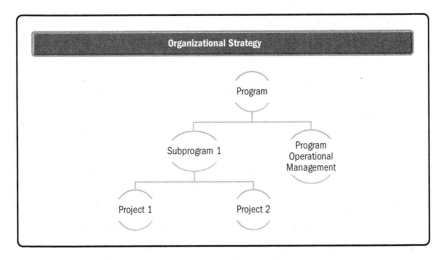

Figure 1-3:   Program structure.

A *project* is a temporary endeavor undertaken to create a unique product, service, or result. The temporary nature of the project indicates that a project has a definite beginning and end.[16] Among numerous examples of projects is a project to improve a specific process, to develop a product or a process, to implement a change, and to implement a new industry standard or regulatory requirement.

A key difference between program management and project management is the strategic focus of programs. Programs are designed to align with organizational strategy and ensure organizational benefits are recognized.[17] We will discuss program strategy alignment in detail in Chapter 3: Program Strategy Alignment.

Using program and project definitions provided above, we can depict program structure, as shown in Figure 1-3.

We can illustrate program structure using a call center's process improvement program as an example. The program goal is to provide the highest call response quality and fastest call response time. The program

---

[16] PMI. (2013). *A guide to the project management body of knowledge (PMBOK® guide)* – Fifth edition. Newtown Square, PA: Author.

[17] Martinelli, R. J., Waddell, J. M., & Rahschulte, T. J. (2014). Transitioning to program management. *PM World (3)*9, 1–3. Retrieved from http://pmworldlibrary.net/wp-content/uploads/2014/09/pmwj26-sep2014-Martinelli-Raschulte-Waddell-Introduction-to-Transitioning-to-program-management.pdf

includes subprogram one, which consists of two projects: Project one improves call response quality, and project two decreases call response time. The program also includes operational management activities, such as setting up program infrastructure, managing program costs and risks, managing links between program components, and coordinating resources across the program.

Programs add value to organizations by delivering a variety of benefits. Examples of benefits include launching new products, developing new and enhancing existing organizational capabilities, facilitating business changes, and implementing process improvements. Programs also realize a benefit of managing related projects as a program, a benefit that cannot be obtained if projects are managed individually.

Program benefits can be realized all at once or in increments, depending on how the projects included in the program deliver their benefits—at once or in phases. An example of a program that realizes benefits at once may be a program to develop a new product; an example of a program that realizes benefits in increments is the call center's process improvement program, which implements process improvement projects in call centers one at a time.

A *portfolio* is a collection of projects, programs, subportfolios, and portfolio operational management activities grouped together to facilitate the effective management of work to meet strategic business objectives.[18] It is important to note that the projects and programs within the portfolio are not always directly related; however, they are linked to the organizational strategic plan using the organizational portfolio. Examples of portfolios may include a process improvement portfolio, a strategic initiatives portfolio, a government programs portfolio, and a market strategies portfolio.

Organizational strategy is the critical force that drives portfolio, program, and project management, and the organizational strategy is a key element that links all three together. However, each of the three— portfolio, program, and project—contributes to the organizational strategy execution in a different way:

- Portfolios select the right programs and projects, prioritizing the work and providing resources;

---

[18] PMI. (2013). *The standard for program management* – Third edition. Newtown Square, PA: Author.

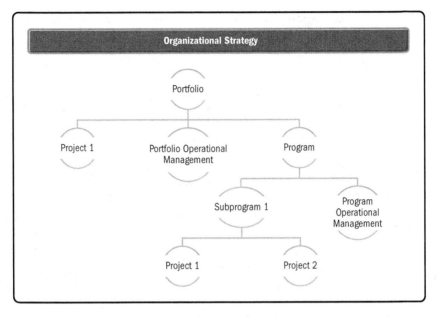

Figure 1-4: Portfolio structure.

- Programs control interdependencies between subprograms and projects; and
- Projects execute specific scope.

Using the definitions above, we can depict portfolio structure, as shown in Figure 1-4.

To successfully manage a program, it is important to clearly understand the differences between portfolio, program, and project management. Table 1-1 compares portfolios, programs, and projects across key dimensions.

Table 1-1 introduced the term *return on investment* (ROI), which is a benefit to an investor, resulting from an investment of some resource.[19] ROI is usually expressed in percentage and is calculated using the following formula:

$$ROI = \left(\frac{Net\ Profit}{Cost\ of\ Investment} \right) \times 100\%$$

---

[19] Return on investment. (n. d.). In *Wikipedia*. Retrieved from https://en.wikipedia.org/wiki/Return_on_investment

Table 1-1: Portfolio, program, and project management comparison across key dimensions within an organization.

	Portfolio	Program	Project
Definition	A collection of projects, programs, subportfolios, and portfolio operational management activities grouped together to facilitate the effective management of work to meet strategic business objectives.	A group of related projects, subprojects, and program operational management activities, managed in a coordinated way to obtain benefits not available from managing them individually.	Temporary endeavor undertaken to create a unique product, service, or result.
Scope	Portfolio scope is an organizational scope, and it may change with the changes in the organization's strategic objectives.	Program scope is large and may change to meet the benefit expectations of the organization.	Project scope is narrow and may be progressively elaborated throughout the project life cycle. The project has defined objectives.
Benefits	Portfolios realize strategic business objectives.	Programs deliver significant benefits.	Projects deliver specific benefits.
Focus	Portfolios focus on grouping that facilitates effective management of work to meet strategic business objectives.	Programs focus on business objectives, value delivery, and benefits management.	Projects focus on executing a sequence of tasks with the objective to deliver defined outcomes and deliverables.
Change	Portfolio manager continually monitors changes in the broad environment.	Program manager anticipates, embraces, and implements changes.	Project manager keeps changes to a minimum.
Planning	Portfolio manager creates and maintains necessary processes and communication about the aggregate portfolio.	Program manager develops the overall program plan and creates high-level plans to guide detailed planning at the component level.	Project manager progressively elaborates high-level information into detailed plans throughout the project life cycle.
Management	Portfolio manager manages portfolio management staff, or program and project management staff, that may have reporting responsibilities into the aggregate portfolio.	Program manager manages program staff and project managers, providing vision and overall leadership.	Project manager manages a project team to meet project objectives.
Monitoring	Portfolio manager monitors strategic changes, aggregate resource allocations, performance results, and portfolio risks.	Program manager monitors program components progress to ensure that overall goals, schedules, and budget are delivered, and program benefits are realized.	Project manager monitors and controls the work of producing services, products, or results that the project is undertaken to deliver.
Success	Success is measured by the aggregate investment performance and benefits realization of the portfolio.	Success is measured by the degree to which the program satisfies the needs and benefits for which it was undertaken. It is also measured by return on investment (ROI), new capabilities, and benefits delivery.	Success is measured by products delivered to specifications, project quality, customer satisfaction, and delivery on time and on budget.

Why Do Organizations Deploy Programs?

Organizations deploy programs to execute organizational strategy. Programs provide a critical link between organizational strategy and its execution. And, through program execution, organizations realize benefits. In this section, we will discuss how to achieve program alignment with the organizational strategy. We also will define program benefits management.

Program Strategy Alignment

Many organizations do not fully understand the value that program management can create and benefits that can be realized through it. Organizations do not always recognize that every strategic initiative is essentially a project or program, and that all strategic changes in an organization occur through projects and programs.[20] That is why program alignment with the organizational strategy is critical for organizational success. And, for organizations to successfully execute strategy through program execution, it is important to understand the value that programs can generate.

As the global advocate for the project, program, and portfolio management profession, PMI has been conducting the *Pulse of the Profession* study since 2006 to provide evidence that implementing strategy successfully is inextricably linked to an organization's capability to deliver successful projects and programs.[21] Organizations that invest in project management waste 13 times less money because their strategic initiatives are completed more successfully. We know project management is essential to any organization's success, yet the message is not being realized.[22]

Organizations achieve program and project strategy alignment by creating a program management office, engaging executive sponsors, and aligning talent management with the organizational strategy.

---

[20] PMI. (2013). *Pulse of the profession®: The high cost of low performance.* Newtown Square, PA: Author.

[21] PMI. (2015). *Pulse of the profession®: Capturing the value of project management.* Newtown Square, PA: Author.

[22] PMI. (2016). *Pulse of the profession®: The high cost of low performance—How will you improve business results?* Newtown Square, PA: Author.

However, more work needs to be done, as program and project management industries' current analysis shows that many programs and projects are not aligned with the organizational strategy. Less than half of organizations report high alignment of projects to organizational strategy.[23] And, there are no published statistics around alignment of programs to organizational strategy. Program strategy alignment will be discussed in detail in Chapter 3: Program Strategy Alignment.

Program Benefits Realization

Benefits realization is a foundational element of program management, as a program should be aimed at the achievement of the anticipated business results. Organizations are more likely to nurture a culture of project management when they fully understand the value it brings and how projects and programs drive change. They also understand that when programs and projects fail, so do profits, because organizations are less likely to achieve strategic goals.[24]

Program management adds business value by serving as the mechanism by which the work of the various operating functions within a company is integrated to create an effective business model. For example, consider the business functions of marketing, engineering, manufacturing, and finance. Each function has its own language and jargon. Marketing language talks about the four Ps (product, price, place, promotion), finance discusses discounted cash flow, engineering discusses technical performance, and manufacturing is interested in production yield and defect rates. To say that experts from different functions often do not understand one another, let alone often do not work well together, is an understatement.

The inclusion of program management in a firm's business model provides value to those organizations seeking to integrate the efforts of their business functions to achieve business results through the development and delivery of new capabilities or transformative change. When program management is properly defined and implemented, it helps to

---

[23] PMI. (2016). *Pulse of the profession®: The high cost of low performance—How will you improve business results?* Newtown Square, PA: Author.

[24] PMI. (2015). *Pulse of the profession®: Capturing the value of project management*. Newtown Square, PA: Author.

execute business strategies through the collective efforts of the business functions of an enterprise.

Program management integrates the collective efforts by focusing the various functions on a common purpose: achievement of improved business results even though they may speak in different jargon; commonality is established with a collective purpose and goal. The integration of cross-organizational efforts increases the probability of successfully achieving the intended business results in a repeatable manner.[25] Program benefits realization will be discussed in more detail in Chapter 4: Program Benefits Realization.

Program Management Performance Domains

In the previous section, we defined programs, projects, and portfolios, and showed relationships among them. We also compared program, project, and portfolio management across key dimensions within the organization. In this section, we will define program management in the broader organizational context and describe how to execute a program by defining and deploying program management performance domains.

Program management performance domains are complementary groupings of related areas of activity, concern, or function that uniquely characterize and differentiate the activities found in one performance domain from the others within the full scope of program management work. Program managers actively carry out work within multiple program management performance domains during all program management phases.[26] There are five program management performance domains (see Figure 1-5):

- Program strategy alignment;
- Program benefits realization;
- Program stakeholder engagement;
- Program governance; and
- Program life cycle management (as in Figure 1-5).

---

[25] Martinelli, R. J., Wadell, J. M., & Rahschulte, T. J. (2014). *Program management for improved business results* (2nd ed.). Hoboken, NJ: Wiley & Sons, Inc.
[26] PMI. (2013). *The standard for program management* – Third edition. Newtown Square, PA: Author.

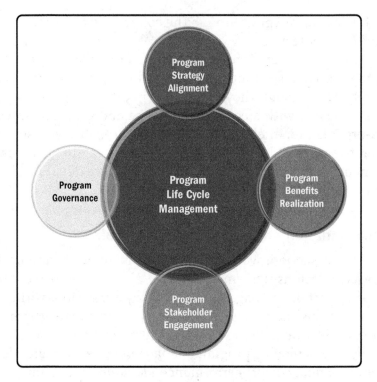

Figure 1-5:   Program management performance domains.

The following are definitions of each performance domain:

- *Program strategy alignment* identifies opportunities and benefits to achieve the organization's strategic objectives through program implementation.
- *Program benefits realization* defines, creates, maximizes, delivers, and sustains the benefits provided by the program.
- *Program stakeholder engagement* captures and understands stakeholder needs, desires, and expectations, and analyzes the impact of the program on the stakeholders, gaining and maintaining stakeholder support, managing stakeholder communications, and mitigating stakeholder resistance.
- *Program governance* establishes processes and procedures for maintaining program management oversight and decision-making support for applicable policies and practices throughout the course of the program.

- *Program life cycle management* manages all of the program activities related to program definition, program benefit delivery, and program closure.[27]

These domains run concurrently during the entire program life cycle. Every program requires some activity in each of the five performance domains. The nature and the complexity of the program determine the degree of activity that a program manager performs within a particular domain. The work performed in each domain is iterative and repeated as needed. A program manager and program team perform tasks within all five domains. And work in these domains is critical to effective and efficient program execution.

Program Life Cycle

Programs are undertaken to deliver benefits by achieving business value and producing anticipated business results. A program has a sponsor who approves funding and assigns a program manager. A program manager integrates and manages multiple subprograms and projects, and handles program operational management activities. To realize program benefits, a program manager executes a program using three phases: definition, benefits delivery, and closure. This set of phases, that are followed to deliver program benefits, is called a *program life cycle.*

Program definition is the first phase of the program life cycle. During this phase, a program sponsor approves program funding and assigns a program manager. A program manager expands the business case and strategic plan objectives, and fully defines expected program outcomes.

Program benefits delivery is a second and iterative phase of the program life cycle. During this phase, a program manager plans, integrates, and manages program components to facilitate delivery of the intended program benefits.

Program closure is the third and last phase of the program life cycle. During this phase, a program manager executes a controlled closure of the program.[28]

---

[27] PMI. (2013). *The standard for program management* – Third edition. Newtown Square, PA: Author.
[28] PMI. (2013). *The standard for program management* – Third edition. Newtown Square, PA: Author.

Figure 1-6:   Program life cycle.

Using the definitions above, the program life cycle and its phases are presented in the graphical image shown in Figure 1-6. We will discuss program life cycle phases in more detail in Chapter 7: Program Life Cycle Management.

The program manager plays a key role throughout the entire program life cycle. Overall, a program manager coordinates and prioritizes resources across components, manages links between components, and manages costs and risks of the program as a whole. However, a program manager role is different during each phase of the program life cycle. Subsequently, a program manager level of oversight, actions, priorities, and hours spent on a program as a whole, and each component within it, vary during each phase.

CHAPTER 2

What Makes a Successful Program Manager?

The program manager is a key driver of a successful program execution. A program manager executes a program by setting up program structure, leading project managers, and delivering program benefits. That is why it is very important to define a program manager role and understand what helps a program manager to succeed in it.

This chapter describes how the organizational structure defines a program manager role. The chapter introduces the program management continuum, a concept that defines four phases within the project-oriented and program-oriented organizational structures. It defines a program manager role in each phase of the program management continuum. The chapter illustrates how program infrastructure enables a program manager to lead. It introduces a proficiency framework examining proficiencies that make a successful program manager. The chapter concludes with a table that compares program, project, and portfolio managers' roles.

The chapter includes the following sections:

- Organizational structure empowers program manager to lead;
- Program manager role;
- Program infrastructure enables program manager to lead;
- Proficiency framework makes a successful program manager; and
- Comparison of the program, project, and portfolio managers' roles.

Organizational Structure Empowers a Program Manager to Lead

Currently, there is a signification variation in how the program management function is utilized across organizations. Some organizations utilize the program management function to its fullest, making it a business extension. While other organizations utilize program management in a limited way, as only administrative or facilitative.

Organizational structure defines how program management is practiced in the organization and defines the role that a program manager plays. We define four types of organizational structures for program management. We also discuss how each of the four types of organizational structures utilizes the program management function and defines a program manager role.

Variation in the program management function drives variation in the program manager role. To understand how different a program manager role can be, it is important to define program management function types and examine how they influence the program manager role.

Some organizations establish their program management function as administration-focused, some as facilitation-focused, and others as integration-focused, and still others as business-focused. This approach to program management within the organizational structure is called the *program management continuum*, and it is graphically displayed in Figure 2-1.[1]

Organizations that fully utilize program management, and often view it as a part of the business management function that provides a link to the organizational strategy, are *program-oriented organizations*. Program-oriented organizations can be either integration-focused or business-focused. In these organizations, a program manager is empowered to deliver business results.

Organizations that do not utilize program management to its full capacity and view program management function only as an extension of the project execution that primarily realizes administrative needs, are

---

[1] Martinelli, R. J., Waddell, J. M., & Rahschulte, T. J. (2014). Transitioning to program management. *PM World Journal, 3*(9), 1–3. Retrieved from http://pmworldlibrary .net/wp-content/uploads/2014/09/pmwj26-sep2014-Martinelli-Raschulte Waddell-Introduction-to-Transitioning-to-program-management.pdf

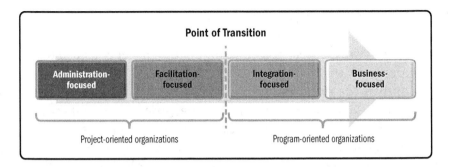

Figure 2-1:   Program management continuum.

project-oriented organizations. Project-oriented organizations can be either administration-focused or facilitation-focused. In these organizations, a program manager role is limited to performing administrative work and executing projects.

Details of the stages of program management continuum reveal different views on—and use of—the program management function as well as show variations in the roles and responsibilities of program managers in each stage.[2]

Project-oriented organizations include:

- *Administration-focused* organizations demonstrate a strong focus on independent projects and provide line management control of the projects. These organizations have a limited program management function, and it is utilized primarily for performing administrative tasks, gathering data, and monitoring activities.
- *Facilitation-focused* organizations are project-oriented. However, projects are grouped into programs, usually organically rather than strategically. Program management serves as a coordination function that facilitates cross-project communication and low-level collaboration.

[2] Martinelli, R. J., Waddell, J. M., & Rahschulte, T. J. (2014). *Program management for improved business results* (2nd ed.). Hoboken, NJ: Wiley & Sons, Inc.

Program-oriented organizations include:

- *Integration-focused* organizations view projects as a part of a program that is driven by organizational strategy. At this point in the continuum, control of the projects shifts from a functional or a line manager to a program manager. The primary focus of program management is integration and synchronization of workflow outcomes and deliverables of multiple projects to create an integrated solution that aligns with organizational strategy.
- *Business-focused* organizations are fully devoted and disciplined in their use of program management practice. Programs are tightly linked to organizational strategy and serve as the strategy implementation mechanism that realizes business goals. In the business-focused culture, organizational hierarchical command and control are replaced by the empowerment and accountability of a program manager.

At the center of the program management continuum, between project-oriented and program-oriented organizations, lies a *point of transition*. This important point represents a decision point where senior leaders make a determined choice to shift their organization from project-oriented to program-oriented.

Organizational structure may limit the program manager role to that of an administrator or a facilitator who executes tasks in the work plan and performs other administrative functions. However, to provide the greatest value to the organization, a program manager must have strong business focus and be able to lead a program relying on in-depth subject matter expertise. Essentially, the program manager needs to operate as the CEO of a program. Integration-focused or business-focused organizational structure supports this role and empowers a program manager to operate at this level.

Senior leadership defines the organizational structure. Changing business needs drive the organizational transition from a project-oriented to a program-oriented structure. Examples of changes include business growth, strategic shifts, changes in the governance structure, and changes in the regulatory and legislative requirements. At the time of the change, organizations assess the current state, and identify gaps between current and future states.

Every organization, whether it is trying to introduce a new or mature existing program management function, has its unique gaps. A *gap* represents a need for an organizational transformation from current to expected program management function. The organization's senior leadership makes a decision to redefine the organizational structure and implement a new structure to better facilitate business needs. In doing so, the organization closes a gap between program management function current and future states.

A key discovery from the program management continuum is the demonstration of what an organization can achieve when it begins to operate as a program-oriented organization. Program strategy alignment strengthens, and the gain in benefits derived from the use of program management increases the further to the right of the program management continuum an organization chooses to operate.[3]

The program management function strengthens, and a program manager role shifts toward higher accountability for achieving business results. A program manager becomes responsible for delivering an integrated solution through program leadership, collaboration with business functions, and coordination of multiple projects within a program, as shown in Figure 2-2. A program manager accomplishes this through effective benefits management, as will be described in Chapter 7: Program Life Cycle Management.

A program manager needs to be fully aware of the organizational structure as it defines a program manager role. A clear understanding of the organizational structure helps a program manager understand expectations for the role and identify opportunities to expand it.

The most effective way of establishing the program management function and defining a program manager role is through an organizational structure. However, significant variations in establishing the program management function and in defining a program management role confirm that, at present, it is not a commonly established practice.

---

[3] Martinelli, R. J., Waddell, J. M., & Rahschulte, T. J. (2014). Transitioning to program management. *PM World Journal, 3*(9), 1–3. Retrieved from http://pmworldlibrary .net/wp-content/uploads/2014/09/pmwj26-sep2014-Martinelli-Raschulte-Waddell-Introduction-to-Transitioning-to-program-management.pdf

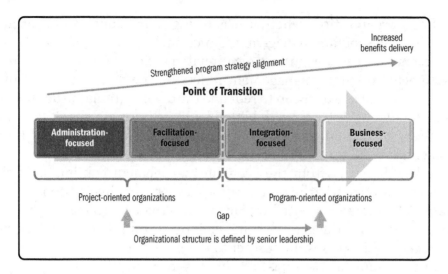

Figure 2-2:   The shift to program-oriented organizations allows organizations to strengthen program strategy alignment and increase benefits delivery.

In some organizations, program managers—and not senior leaders—establish program management functions and define the program manager role. Frequently, a program manager role is dependent upon the ability of the person serving in it. As a result, program manager success cannot be replicated, and the role has to be redefined if a program manager leaves. All of the above contributes to a significant existing variation in the program manager role that exists not only between organizations, but sometimes even between different departments within the same organization.

In project-oriented organizations, a program manager can help influence a shift to program-oriented organizations, and, in the organizations where the program management function is not clearly defined, a program manager can help structure it. One of the venues through which a program manager can help define the program management function and structure a program manager role is the program management community of practice (PgMCoP), described in Chapter 11: Program Management Community of Practice.

Program Manager Role

The program management function defines the program manager role. The program management continuum identifies four types of program

Table 2-1: The roles of a program manager in each phase of the program management continuum.

	Administrative-Focused	Facilitation-Focused	Integration-Focused	Business-Focused
Role	In a project-oriented organization, a program manager performs the roles of an administrator and a facilitator.		In a program-oriented organization, a program manager performs the role of a business manager.	
Focus	A program manager fulfills an administrative role that includes taking notes, scheduling meetings, gathering data, and monitoring activities.	A program manager facilitates cross-project communication and low-level collaboration.	A program manager is focused on integration and synchronization of workflow outcomes and multiple project deliverables to create an integrated solution that aligns with the organizational strategy.	A program manager is empowered to lead a program and is held accountable for its execution. A program manager is a business manager, subject matter expert (SME), and a primary point of customer contact. A program manager has profit-and-loss responsibility for the client-engaged program.

management functions, each of which defines a program manager role differently. Let us examine these roles closely by comparing them in Table 2-1.

To provide the greatest value to the organization, the program management function must be established as having a strong business focus.[4] To achieve this organizational structure of a program-oriented enterprise, a program manager role should have the following responsibilities:

- Develop program plan and budget;
- Be accountable for program execution, including program schedule, budget, and quality;
- Review and approve project plans for conformance with program strategy, program plan, and schedule;
- Act as the communications conduit with executive sponsors and the program steering committee, and conduct periodic briefings and status updates; and
- Escalate decisions and risks to executive sponsors.

---

[4] Martinelli, R. J., Waddell, J. M., & Rahschulte, T. J. (2014). Transitioning to program management. *PM World Journal, 3*(9), 1–3. Retrieved from http://pmworldlibrary.net/wp-content/uploads/2014/09/pmwj26-sep2014-Martinelli-Raschulte-Waddell-Introduction-to-Transitioning-to-program-management.pdf

A successful program manager is a business leader who understands the role, business environment, stakeholders, regulatory requirements, and more. A program manager is not an administrator or a facilitator who simply executes the work plan.

When organizations shift from project-oriented to program-oriented, there is a subsequent shift in the program manager role from administration-focused to business-focused, potentially leading to gaps in knowledge, skills, and experience. To close these gaps and facilitate the transition, organizations have to provide training to program managers. Program managers should assist with identifying gaps between current and future requirements, and identify training needs to close the gaps. One of the venues through which program managers can assist in this process is the program management community of practice (PgMCoP), which will be described in Chapter 11: Program Management Community of Practice.

Program Infrastructure Enables a Program Manager to Lead

The program manager's ability to lead a program is dependent on infrastructure (e.g., a system that supports the program management function, a status reporting tool that aids in monitoring program health, and a financial tool that assists in monitoring program financial health). Infrastructure enables a program manager to execute program operational management tasks quicker, focusing the majority of time on leading a program, delivering its strategic objectives, becoming a trusted advisor, and acting as a subject matter expert (SME).

Program infrastructure should include a plan that allows aggregating project information into a program. The plan can either be Microsoft Project, a spreadsheet, or a database. The system should have the ability to aggregate from multiple projects into program tasks and milestones.[5]

A program manager should utilize a wide set of tools, including status reports, time lines, resource utilization reports, risk reports, and financial

---

[5] Blomquist, T., & Müller, R. (2004). *Program and portfolio managers: Analysis of roles and responsibilities.* Proceedings of the PMI Research Conference (11–14 July), London, England.

health reports. Program management system support and financial and status reporting tools will be described in detail in Chapter 8: Program Management Infrastructure.

A business-focused program manager should spend about 60% of the time leading a program, and the remaining 40% of the time executing program operational management tasks. This breakdown is possible if a program manager can operate as a business program manager and has effective program infrastructure.

If, due to infrastructure limitations, a program manager spends more than 40% of the time executing program operational management tasks, a program manager cannot lead a program effectively. That is why, at the start of a program, a program manager should assess system capabilities and tools, and determine if they enable effective program management. If a program manager does not have sufficient infrastructure available, a program manager should work with the organizational leadership and professional peers to enhance infrastructure. One of the venues through which a program manager can advocate for system implementation or an upgrade, and get support in developing new and updating existing tools, is the program management community of practice (PgMCoP), which will be described in Chapter 11: Program Management Community of Practice.

Proficiency Framework Makes a Successful Program Manager

In the preceding sections, we have concluded that a program-oriented organization empowers a program manager to lead. We also determined that program infrastructure enables a program manager to lead. In this section, we will review a program proficiency framework that makes a successful program manager.

For many project managers, the next move in their careers is the step up to program manager. Many practitioners lack a true understanding of the role and the skills required to make the transition. Program managers are not simply senior project managers.[6]

---

[6] PMI. (2010). *What does it take to be a program manager? Established veterans advise up-and-coming project managers on how to make the jump to program manager.* Newtown Square, PA: Author.

To help illustrate the differences between program manager and project manager roles, we will compare role definitions. *Program managers* coordinate groups of related projects rather than manage individual projects themselves.[7] *Project managers* are change agents: They make project goals their own and use their skills and expertise to inspire a sense of shared purpose within the project team.[8] Role definition comparison illustrates that a program manager role is larger in scope, broader in the framework, and more complex in content than a project manager role is.

Programs differ from projects in an important way; programs need to be managed in a way that enables them to readily adapt to the uncertainty of their outcomes and to the unpredictability of the environment in which they operate. This need influences the proficiencies required of a program manager. To manage a program effectively, program managers need to blend control-oriented leadership and management skills that support execution of the program and its components.[9] To succeed in this complex environment, a program manager needs to have various program management proficiencies.

As an organization moves from project-oriented to program-oriented, a program manager spends more time leading a program and less time executing it. Leading a program includes leading a program team, engaging leadership, integrating program work, connecting cross-functional interdependencies, and proactively identifying risks. Executing a program includes completing program operational tasks, updating status reporting, tracking and resolving risks, updating the program management plan, and setting program meeting cadence.

An administration-focused program manager operating in a project-oriented organization spends the entire time executing program operational tasks, with the key one being monitoring the program plan. A facilitation-focused program manager operating in project-oriented organizations spends about 20% of the time leading

---

[7] PMI. (2008). *The standard for program management* – Second edition. Newtown Square, PA: Author.
[8] PMI. (2017). *Who are project managers?* Retrieved from https://www.pmi.org /about/learn-about-pmi/who-are-project-managers
[9] PMI (2013). *The standard for program management* – Third edition. Newtown Square, PA: Author.

a program by facilitating low-level collaboration, and 80% of the time executing it.

Once an organization crosses the center of the continuum, a program manager becomes responsible for ensuring that cross-project interdependencies are managed and synchronized. Because of this responsibility, a program manager has to lead the team in their integration effort. In a program-oriented organization, leading a program becomes a more complex effort, as program teams are larger than project teams and, at times, are spread out geographically. Program structure becomes more complex, leading to a multifaceted business governance structure. All these changes require a program manager to spend more time leading a program. That is why program manager proficiencies expand when moving to the right of the program management continuum, enabling a program manager to operate as a business-focused program manager.

An integration-focused program manager operating in program-oriented organizations spends 60% of the time leading a program, including providing cross-project communication and ensuring the cross-project interdependencies are managed and synchronized, and 40% of the time executing a program.

A business-focused program manager operating in program-focused organizations spends 80% of the time leading a program and 20% of the time executing it.[10] An experienced business program manager operating in a program-focused organization confirmed that he spends 80% of the time leading a program and 20% of the time executing it. The split between program leadership and program execution is achieved by employing an excellent team of project managers, who work the details of a given project within a program. However, there are times when a program manager needs to drop down into the operational details of a given component to troubleshoot, provide guidance, or work through some technical details.[11]

---

[10] Written in collaboration with Russ Martinelli, co-author of the book, *Program management for improved business results.* (2014). Hoboken, NJ: John Wiley & Sons, Inc.

[11] Lovelace, J. (2016). *Interview.* MsPM, PMP, PgMP, Product Launch Management Advisor at Eli Lilly and Company.

The program management continuum graphically shows the percentage of time that program managers spend leading a program and the percentage of time that they spend executing program management operational tasks in each stage, as shown in Figure 2-3.

We developed a program proficiency framework that defines proficiencies that allow a program manager to succeed in leading and executing a program. The proficiency framework groups program proficiencies into three major categories (see Figure 2-4):

- Program leadership;
- Program operational management; and
- Interpersonal skills.

Program Leadership Proficiency

Program leadership proficiency includes:

- Gain in-depth program content knowledge;
- Be aware of the organizational structure;
- Know organizational strategy; and
- Manage stakeholders.

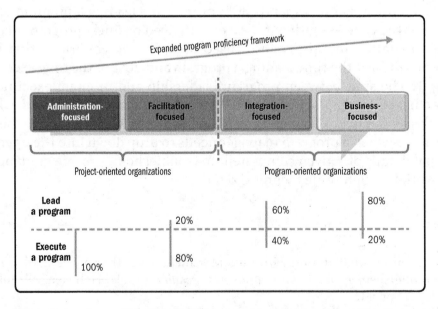

Figure 2-3:   Percentage of weekly time program managers spend leading and executing a program in each stage of the program management continuum.

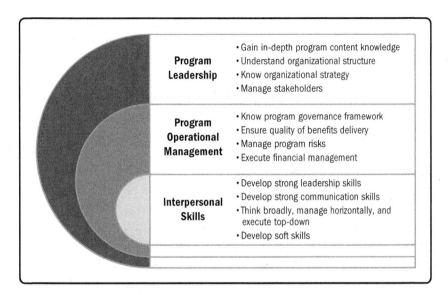

Program Leadership	• Gain in-depth program content knowledge • Understand organizational structure • Know organizational strategy • Manage stakeholders	
Program Operational Management	• Know program governance framework • Ensure quality of benefits delivery • Manage program risks • Execute financial management	
Interpersonal Skills	• Develop strong leadership skills • Develop strong communication skills • Think broadly, manage horizontally, and execute top-down • Develop soft skills	

Figure 2-4: Program proficiency framework.

Gain In-Depth Program Content Knowledge

Program content knowledge is essential for successful program execution, as it serves as a keystone for program leadership and program operational management. A program manager needs to develop content knowledge to lead a program successfully, fully realize program benefits, manage cross-functional interdependencies, and be able to identify program and component risks proactively.

Program content knowledge includes an in-depth understanding of a product or a service that a program is developing, who are the customers for it, how the customers will use a product or a service, what the market characteristics are, who the competitors in the market are, and what the market trends and best practices are. Using program content knowledge, a program manager can maximize program benefits realization.

Using the call center's process improvement program example, we will illustrate the importance of program content knowledge in successful program execution. A successful program manager needs to have a fundamental knowledge of services that call centers provide and an understanding of customers who use these services. A program manager also needs to know the market in which call centers operate, competitors in the market, market trends, and the call center's best practices. Bringing this knowledge together, a program manager can improve the call center's processes, ensuring a high level of customer satisfaction and the call center's competitive market position, as well as defining new industry best practices.

The need to have program content knowledge increases as organizations become program-oriented. In-depth program content knowledge is one of the key proficiencies that a program manager needs to master to become successful as a business program manager or a program CEO. To add to program content knowledge, a program manager may engage subject matter experts (SMEs) and business owners.

Understand Organizational Structure

A program manager needs to understand organizational structure, as it defines the program management function that, in turn, defines a program manager role. As was discussed earlier, the business-focused program management function empowers a program manager to lead, while the administration-focused program management function limits the program manager role to administrative functions. A project manager is not required to be aware of the organizational structure.

Know Organizational Strategy

The program manager is required to think strategically to align the program and its constituent projects to the strategic business goals of the organization. This includes understanding how a firm or organization performs strategic planning, and being able to separate aspects of strategic thinking from tactical and operational elements as the need arises. A part of strategic thinking involves a basic understanding of the industry in which a business operates and of how the firm's strategy fits with the direction of the industry long term.[12]

A program manager needs to know the organizational strategy. A program manager employs strategic vision and planning to align program goals and benefits with long-term organizational goals. Once the program goals and benefits are defined, a program manager develops a program management plan to execute program components. The program manager is responsible for ensuring alignment of the individual plans with the program goals and benefits.[13]

---

[12] Martinelli, R. J., Waddell, J. M., & Rahschulte, T. J. (2014). *Program management for improved business results.* (2nd ed.). Hoboken, NJ: John Wiley & Sons, Inc.
[13] PMI. (2013). *The standard for program management* – Third edition. Newtown Square, PA: Author.

A program manager needs to observe shifts in organizational strategy to be able to realign a program and components with the changed strategy. A project manager is not required to be knowledgeable about the organizational strategy, as a program manager realigns program components with the changed strategy.

Manage Stakeholders

Stakeholder management skills are critical for program manager success. The program manager first must know how to determine the organizational landscape in which the program is to operate. He or she will likely have many stakeholders, both internal and external to the organization, who need to be influenced.[14]

It is important to initiate, engage, and maintain stakeholder relationships to manage the program and achieve desired benefits effectively. Active stakeholder engagement helps build and maintain ongoing support of the program. The program manager should identify stakeholders, understand their needs and expectations, develop a stakeholder management plan to support stakeholders, and help align their expectations. The program manager should recognize the dynamic human aspects of each program stakeholder's expectations and manage accordingly.[15]

Program Operational Management Proficiency

Program operational management proficiency includes:
- Knowing the program governance framework;
- Ensuring the quality of benefits delivery;
- Managing program risks; and
- Executing financial management.

Knowing Program Governance Framework

Program manager proficiencies should include knowledge of establishing and executing the program governance framework. Within a program, a program manager should identify work that is required,

---

[14] Martinelli, R. J., Waddell, J. M., & Rahschulte, T. J. (2014). *Program management for improved business results.* (2nd ed.). Hoboken, NJ: John Wiley & Sons, Inc.
[15] PMI. (2013). *The standard for program management* – Third edition. Newtown Square, PA: Author.

build the program management plan, and allocate and optimize resources across all components.

A program manager should define the pacing of components and obtain incremental benefits before the program is complete. While focusing on benefits delivery, a program manager needs to adjust the pacing of components to ensure benefits quality. A project manager defines the pacing of a component on a smaller scale.

Ensuring Quality of Benefits Delivery

The program manager, as the quality champion of his or her program's customers, needs to ensure the program results meet or exceed the quality expectations of the customer. The program manager should possess a bias of action, be able to think globally, and assure that quality, reliability, manufacturability, serviceability, and regulatory compliance objectives are achieved.[16]

A program manager should compare delivered benefits to the program charter to ensure that the intended and delivered benefits match. Utilizing program content knowledge, a program manager needs to question the content (e.g., will the solution deliver the intended benefits?). It is important to have quality metrics to ensure that the program delivered benefits as defined in the business case. Quality metrics tools can aid in measuring the quality of the benefits, as will be described in Chapter 8: Program Management Infrastructure.

Managing Program Risks

A program manager needs to be able to identify program and component risks proactively. In-depth knowledge of the program content is a key to the program manager's ability to identify and manage risks. The program manager also needs to be able to shift focus between components to give attention to critical risks. A program manager can utilize a program risk-tracking tool to aid with tracking and resolution of program issues. We will discuss the tool in detail in Chapter 8: Program Management Infrastructure.

---

[16] Martinelli, R. J., Waddell, J. M., & Rahschulte, T. J. (2014). *Program management for improved business results.* (2nd ed.). Hoboken, NJ: John Wiley & Sons, Inc.

Executing Financial Management

To be successful from a business perspective, the program manager must possess sufficient business skills to understand the organization's business model and financial goals. This requires that a program manager can develop a comprehensive program business case that supports the company's objectives and strategies, the ability to manage the program within the business aspects of the company, and the ability to understand and analyze related financial measures about the program.[17]

Programs have significantly larger budgets than projects have. The program budget also often includes expenses and capital expenditures, while the project budget often includes only expenses. So, to be able to execute a program on budget, a program manager needs to have advanced knowledge of financial management and budgeting. Additionally, to be able to identify, investigate, and resolve any variances between the program budget and actuals, a program manager needs to be able to perform a variance analysis. Variance analysis will be described in Chapter 8: Program Management Infrastructure. A project manager also needs to have a knowledge of financial management and budgeting. However, a project manager applies this knowledge on a smaller scale of an individual project.

Interpersonal Skills

Programs frequently operate in a matrix organization. A *matrix organization* is defined as one in which there is dual or multiple managerial accountability and responsibility. In a matrix, there are usually two chains of command, one along functional lines and the other along the project, product, or client lines.[18] In a matrix organization, program team members do not report directly to a program manager, and team members frequently work on more than one project or a program at a time. The complex program environment calls for a program manager to have strong interpersonal skills. Using the call center's process improvement

---

[17] Martinelli, R. J., Waddell, J. M., & Rahschulte, T. J. (2014). *Program management for improved business results.* (2nd ed.). Hoboken, NJ: John Wiley & Sons, Inc.
[18] Stuckenbruck, L. C. (1979, September). The matrix organization. *Project Management Quarterly.* Retrieved from https://www.pmi.org/learning/library/matrix-organization-structure-reason-evolution-1837

program example, we will illustrate that a complex program environment requires a program manager to have strong interpersonal skills.

The call center's process improvement program team includes project managers for process improvement projects one and two, and the call center's directors. Project managers work in the project management organization, where they manage one or more projects. Project managers are also responsible for the execution of process improvement projects one and two. Call center directors work in the call centers, where they are responsible for their daily operations. Call center directors are responsible for the process improvement program implementation in their call centers.

To successfully execute the call center's process improvement program, a program manager needs to bring the team together under the common goal of realizing the call center's process improvement program benefits. A program manager can do that by developing a variety of interpersonal skills that help them succeed in the complex program environment, including:

- Developing strong leadership skills;
- Developing strong communication skills;
- Thinking broadly, horizontally, and top-down; and
- Developing soft skills.

Developing Strong Leadership Skills

A program manager needs to have the capability to build, coalesce, and champion the team to deliver a solution that will satisfy the company's goals and the customer's needs.[19]

A program manager should develop strong leadership skills to lead programs throughout the program life cycle. A program manager leads the program management team in establishing program direction, identifying interdependencies, communicating program requirements, tracking progress, making decisions, identifying and mitigating risks, and resolving conflicts and issues. A program manager works with project managers and functional managers to gain support, resolve conflicts,

---

[19] Martinelli, R. J., Waddell, J. M., Rahschulte, T. J. (2014). *Program management for improved business results*. (2nd ed.). Hoboken, NJ: John Wiley & Sons, Inc.

and direct individual program team members by providing specific work instructions.[20]

Today's business models have created additional team-building challenges for program managers. It is common for program team members to be distributed across multiple countries. Skills for managing virtual teams have become an emerging critical skill for program managers. There are many aspects to successfully leading a geographically distributed or virtual team.

Leading a virtual program team raises the following question: Is it possible to build true leadership in virtual teams when members are geographically, culturally, organizationally, and time-zone dispersed? Industry expert Patrick Little, a senior IT program manager for a leading research hospital, states that leading a virtual team is possible, but it takes additional effort from all members of the team. Leadership responsibilities include motivating, seeking information and opinions, mediating, facilitating communication, removing barriers, lubricating interfaces, and making each conflict functional so it can be used to improve the quality of our decisions.[21]

Developing Strong Communication Skills

A program manager needs to have strong communication skills to communicate effectively with various program stakeholders, including sponsors, customers, vendors, and executives. More specifically, a program manager needs to be able to pivot and communicate upward, across, and downward, including:

- Upward externally to the government, industry, and investors;
- Upward internally to the program sponsor and organization executives;
- Across externally to the vendors and customers;
- Across internally to the multiple departments within the organization; and
- Downward to subprogram and project managers.

---

[20] PMI. (2013). *The standard for program management* – Third edition. Newtown Square, PA: Author.

[21] Martinelli, R. J., Waddell, J. M., & Rahschulte, T. J. (2014). *Program management for improved business results.* (2nd ed.). Hoboken, NJ: John Wiley & Sons, Inc.

Effective communication requires the ability to speak multiple disciplinary languages—business language when communicating with senior management, user language when communicating with the customers, technology language when communicating with technologists, and so on. Effective communication skills also mean that the program manager should be able to actively listen and provide clarity in difficult situations, many times serving as the translator in multidisciplinary discussions. The program manager must be able to use and extend stakeholders' knowledge to develop the ability to choose the right model of communication to address customers, senior management, team members, suppliers, and others. This involves knowing when to see people face-to-face, when to send messages, and when to avoid them altogether.[22] And finally, they must effectively communicate, with skills that include being able to write powerful messages to various program stakeholders.

To ensure timely communication with stakeholders, a program manager needs to determine communication frequency. The program management communication plan should address stakeholder needs and expectations, as well as provide key messages promptly and in a format designed specifically for the target audience, as will be described in Chapter 8: Program Management Infrastructure.

Don't wait for stakeholders to read their report and react. As you get to know their habits, you will learn that some need a phone call or targeted email to draw their attention.[23] A program manager needs to learn stakeholder habits and work styles and be able to customize program communication plan execution to stakeholder needs.

Think Broadly, Manage Horizontally, and Execute Top-Down

A successful program manager needs to operate on different levels, including thinking broadly, managing horizontally, and executing top-down:

- Think broadly to integrate program components, however be in the low-enough level of details to proactively identify program and component risks;

---

[22] Martinelli, R. J., Waddell, J. M., & Rahschulte, T. J. (2014). *Program management for improved business results.* (2nd ed.). Hoboken, NJ: John Wiley & Sons, Inc.
[23] Merrick, A. (2015). *Allied forces.* Retrieved from http://www.pmi.org/-/media/pmi/landing-pages/business-analysis-tools-silverpop/pdf/allied-forces-project-management-business-analysis.pdf

- Manage horizontally and ensure that the cross-component work effort remains feasible from a business standpoint and realizes benefits; and
- Execute top-down by implementing structure on a program level and executing it on a component level.

In program management, delivering the whole solution is a primary means of achieving customer satisfaction. The program manager needs to be able to demonstrate a commitment to the customer and demonstrate knowledge of customer application and needs. Those skilled in systems thinking can view projects and activities from a broad perspective that includes seeing overall characteristics and patterns rather than just individual elements. By focusing on the entirety of the program, or in essence, the system aspects of the program (inputs, outputs, and inter-relationships), the program manager improves the probability of delivering the whole solution and meeting the expectations of the customer. This involves the ability to see the big picture, crossing boundaries, and being able to combine disparate elements into a holistic entity. Usually this ability resides in people with diverse backgrounds, multidisciplined minds, and a broad spectrum of experiences.[24]

A program manager needs to think broadly to be able to integrate multiple program components together as a package. Additionally, a program manager needs to communicate program vision and articulate benefits of the program oversight. At the same time, a program manager should be engaged in the low-enough level of details to be able to identify program and component risks. In contrast, a project manager has a narrow focus on the project at hand.

The program manager manages horizontally across the functional projects involved with the program. The program manager ensures that the cross-project work effort remains feasible from a business standpoint and realizes benefits. The goal is to leverage return on investment and control not available from managing projects separately, helping organizations to achieve strategic results. In contrast, the project manager manages only vertically.[25]

---

[24] Martinelli, R. J., Waddell, J. M., & Rahschulte, T. J. (2014). *Program management for improved business results.* (2nd ed.). Hoboken, NJ: John Wiley & Sons, Inc.
[25] PMI. (2010). *What does it take to be a program manager? Established veterans advise up-and-coming project managers on how to make the jump to program manager.*

A program manager drives a program to execution using a top-down approach that includes setting up the program structure and implementing it on a program level, and executing it on a component level. If the structure is not working at the component level, a program manager implements changes on a program level and cascades them down to the component level. In contrast, a project manager applies the bottom-up approach to project management by planning and executing project phases.

Developing Soft Skills

As was mentioned earlier, a program team usually includes members from different departments within the organization who rarely report directly to a program manager. To successfully lead a team, a program manager needs to have soft skills, including an ability to influence, prioritize work, facilitate, trust instincts, push back, and be politically savvy.

Influencing

The influencing traits of a strong program manager include being socially adept in interacting with others in any given situation, having the ability to assess all aspects of information and behavior without passing judgment or injecting bias, and being able to effectively communicate your point of view to change an opinion or change the course of action.[26]

A program manager leading a virtual team operates in the environment with no physical and social presence, and faces the additional challenges of cultural and language barriers. To be able to influence in the virtual program environment, a program manager needs to have a high level of emotional intelligence. A program manager needs to be able to read between the lines and be aware of the virtual team dynamics. And, through effective communication, a program manager needs to influence decisions and motivate a program team.

Prioritizing

Prioritization of work begins with program core assumptions validation with the stakeholders and program governance body. If assumptions are incorrect, it is possible that program priorities will be incorrect. For example,

---

[26] Martinelli, R. J., Waddell, J. M., & Rahschulte, T. J. (2014). *Program management for improved business results.* (2nd ed.). Hoboken, NJ: John Wiley & Sons, Inc.

if cost containment is the highest priority for a program, then a program manager must be emphatic about staying within the financial constraints. If technological leadership is the highest priority, a program manager needs to keep the team focused on technical aspects of a program. The ability of a program manager to focus project team work on the highest priority for a program is crucial for delivering intended program benefits.

Often, team members manage multiple, and sometimes conflicting, priorities. A program manager needs to be able to prioritize work for himself or herself and the team members. As programs often have a complex structure, a program manager needs to ensure that the time is spent on value-added work and the waste is minimized.

Facilitating

A program manager needs to have good facilitation skills to help multiple stakeholders, customers, clients, and team members to communicate and collaborate effectively. Good facilitation skills help to ensure that relationships between team members occur as needed—productively. Core facilitation skills include the ability to draw out varying opinions and viewpoints among team members to create a discussion and collaboration boundaries, and to summarize and synthesize details into useful information and strategy. Other beneficial facilitation skills include using personal energy to maintain forward momentum, being able to rationalize cause and effect, and helping team members stay focused on the primary topics of discussion and collaboration.[27]

Trusting Your Instinct

Among the valuable soft skills that a program manager should develop is the ability to trust your instinct. Ralph Waldo Emerson said, "Trust your instinct to the end, though you can render no reason." In simplified terms, if you feel that something is wrong, it probably is. For example, if requirements review shows incompleteness that may result in failure during execution, start by conducting a detailed review. And, if an initial conclusion about requirements incompleteness is confirmed, revert by bringing the team back to the drawing board. Ability to trust your instinct is based on the program content knowledge.

---

[27] Martinelli, R. J., Waddell, J. M., & Rahschulte, T. J. (2014). *Program management for improved business results.* (2nd ed.). Hoboken, NJ: John Wiley & Sons, Inc.

Pushback

While executing a program, a program manager may come across situations that require pushing back. Power to push back on something that does not seem right should be based on in-depth program content knowledge. An example may be a need to push back on approval of a document if it does not meet quality standards or has incomplete content.

Being Politically Savvy

In addition to understanding the organizational structure, the program manager needs to be politically savvy to navigate politics within it effectively. Company politics are a natural part of any organization, and the program manager should understand that politics is a behavioral aspect of program management that he or she must contend with to succeed. The key is not to be naïve and to understand that not every program stakeholder sees great value in the program. A program manager must be politically sensible by being sensitive to the interests of the most powerful stakeholders, and at the same time, demonstrate good judgment by acting with integrity. The program manager must actively manage the politics surrounding his or her program to protect against negative effects of political maneuvering on the part of stakeholders and to exploit politically advantageous situations. To do this, it is important that the program manager possesses both a keen understanding of the organization and the political savvy necessary to build strong relationships to leverage and influence the power base of the company effectively.[28]

Proficiencies Align With the Organizational Structure

The skills and competencies of a company's program managers need to align with how program management is implemented and the roles they are expected to perform.[29] Organizational structure defines the program manager role and, subsequently, the proficiencies needed to be successful in it. In a project-oriented organization, a program manager mostly has an administrative or facilitative role. In this role, a program manager spends, at most, 20% of the time leading a program, and

---

[28] Martinelli, R. J., Waddell, J. M., & Rahschulte, T. J. (2014). *Program management for improved business results.* (2nd ed.). Hoboken, NJ: John Wiley & Sons, Inc.

[29] Martinelli, R. J., Waddell, J. M., & Rahschulte, T. J. (2014). *Program management for improved business results.* (2nd ed.). Hoboken, NJ: John Wiley & Sons, Inc.

between 80% and 100% of the time executing program operational management tasks. Proficiencies required for this role are limited and do not include all listed in the program proficiency framework.

If an organization becomes program-oriented, a program manager role expands, requiring additional proficiencies to support the transition from administration-focused to business-focused program management. In the program-oriented structure, a program manager has an integration or business role. In this role, a program manager spends 60% to 80% of the time leading a program and 20% to 40% of the time executing program operational management tasks. To succeed in this role, a program manager needs to develop all proficiencies included in the program proficiency framework.

We will examine how proficiencies in the program proficiency framework change between project-oriented and program-oriented organizations, as outlined in Table 2-2. We will describe proficiency level using the following ranking: none, basic, limited, good, and excellent.

Organizations can strengthen program strategy alignment and increase benefits delivery as the program management function moves to the right along the program management continuum toward the program-oriented organization. Programs are tightly linked to organizational business strategy and serve as the strategy implementation mechanism to realize the business goals. In the business-focused culture, organizational hierarchical command and control are replaced by empowerment and accountability on the part of the program manager.[30]

A program manager's ability to lead a program is dependent on program infrastructure, (e.g., a system that supports program management, and tools that aid in monitoring program health). Program infrastructure enables a program manager to execute program operational management tasks quicker, focusing the majority of the time on leading a program, delivering to the strategic objectives, and becoming a trusted advisor and a subject matter expert.

---

[30] Martinelli, R. J., Waddell, J. M., & Rahschulte, T. J. (2014). Transitioning to program management. *PM World Journal, 3*(9), 1–3. Retrieved from http://pmworldlibrary.net/wp-content/uploads/2014/09/pmwj26-sep2014 -Martinelli-Raschulte-Waddell-Introduction-to-Transitioning-to-program -management.pdf

Table 2-2: Proficiencies in the program proficiency framework expand as an organization moves from project-oriented to program-oriented.

Proficiency Area	Proficiencies	Project-Oriented Organizations		Program-Oriented Organizations	
		Administration-focused	Facilitation-focused	Integration-focused	Business-focused
Leadership	**Weekly time allocation in percentage**	**0%**	**20%**	**40%**	**60%**
	Gain deep program content knowledge	Basic program content knowledge	Limited program content knowledge; helps facilitate cross-project collaboration	Good program content knowledge; ensures integrated solution delivery	Excellent program content knowledge; warrants program alignment with organizational strategy
	Be aware of organizational structure	None	Basic familiarity with organizational structure	Limited knowledge of organizational structure and its impact on program manager role	Excellent knowledge of organizational structure and how it defines program manager role
	Know organizational strategy	None	Basic familiarity with organizational strategy	Limited knowledge of organizational strategy and understanding of how a program aligns with it	Excellent knowledge of organizational strategy and assurance of full program alignment with it
	Manage stakeholders	None	Basic executive sponsor management skills	Good organizational leadership and program sponsor management skills	Excellent internal and external stakeholder management skills
Program Management	**Weekly time allocation in percentage**	**100%**	**80%**	**60%**	**40%**
	Know program governance framework	None	Basic knowledge of program governance framework to ensure low-level, cross-project collaboration	Good knowledge of program governance framework to ensure an integrated solution	Excellent knowledge of program governance framework, and ability to establish and execute it
	Ensure quality of benefits delivery	None	Basic quality assurance across projects	Limited quality assurance of integrated solution	Excellent quality assurance of program benefits delivery
	Manage program risks	None	Basic program risk management skills	Limited risk identification and management skills	Excellent risk management skills, including foreseeing and managing risks, and shifting focus to the critical risks

Proficiency Area	Proficiencies	Project-Oriented Organizations		Program-Oriented Organizations	
		Administration-focused	Facilitation-focused	Integration-focused	Business-focused
	Execute financial management	None	Basic financial management skills, including setting up a budget and tracking actual spending	Good financial management skills, including setting up a budget and tracking actual spending	Excellent financial management skills, including setting up a budget, performing monthly forecasts, tracking actual spending, conducting variance analysis, and proactively managing financial issues
Interpersonal Skills	Develop strong leadership skills	None	Limited leadership skills to ensure cross-project collaboration	Good leadership skills to ensure work synchronization and integrated solution delivery	Excellent leadership skills to build and lead a team, and empower team members
	Develop strong communication skills	Basic program communication skills	Limited communication skills, including communication with program team and program sponsor	Good communication skills, including communication with program sponsor, stakeholders, organizational leadership, and program team	Excellent communication skills, including communicating internally and externally, upward, across, and downward.
	Think broadly, manage horizontally, and execute top-down	None	Basic ability to think broadly to ensure cross-project collaboration	Limited ability to think broadly and manage horizontally to ensure integrated solution delivery	Excellent ability to think broadly, manage horizontally, and execute top-down to realize business goals
	Develop soft skills	Basic interpersonal skills	Limited ability to influence and facilitate	Good ability to influence, facilitate, and prioritize work	Excellent ability to influence, facilitate, prioritize work, trust your instincts, be able to push back, and be politically savvy

As the organization moves from project-oriented to program-oriented, a program manager spends more time leading a program and less time executing program operational management tasks. To succeed in the complex organizational environment, a program manager needs to have various program proficiencies, and program proficiencies expand when organizations move from a project-oriented to a program-oriented structure, enabling a program manager to operate as a business program manager or a program CEO.

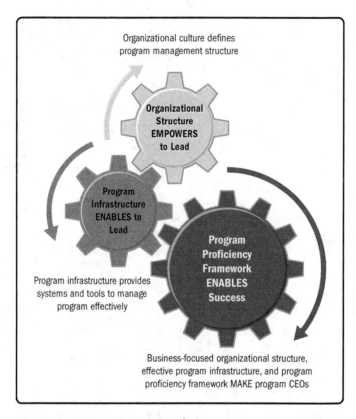

Figure 2-5: Organizational structure empowers to lead, program infrastructure enables to lead, and program proficiency framework enables success, making a program CEO.

A program typically has a large and complex structure that includes multiple components. A program manager also manages the expectations of external and internal stakeholders. To operate as a program CEO, a program manager needs to have three main modules, which include an organizational structure that empowers program managers to lead, a program infrastructure that enables a program manager to lead, and a program proficiency framework that enables a program manager to succeed, as shown in Figure 2-5.

Comparison of Program, Project, and Portfolio Manager Roles

A program manager needs to clearly understand his or her role as well as the roles of portfolio and project managers. Understanding each of these roles is critical for achieving the successful collaboration necessary to maximize program benefits.

In the preceding sections, we defined a program manager role, examined what empowers a program manager to lead, what enables him or her to lead, and recorded a program proficiency framework that enables a program manager to succeed. Now, we will compare the program manager role with portfolio and project manager roles to gain a clear understanding of what each role does and how these roles interact.

Using the call center's process improvement program as an example, we will illustrate the relationship between a program, portfolio, and project. The call center's process improvement program is set to improve call response quality and decrease call response time. The program structure includes subprogram one, which consists of two projects: Project one improves call response quality, and project two decreases call response time. The program also has an implementation project three: Implement projects one and two in all call centers. Additionally, the program includes operational management activities, such as manage program costs and risks, manage links between projects, and coordinate and prioritize resources across projects.

The call center's process improvement program is included in their portfolio. The portfolio executes the process improvement program and conducts the call center's audit. And, similarly to the program operational management activities, the portfolio has operational management activities, as shown in Figure 2-6.

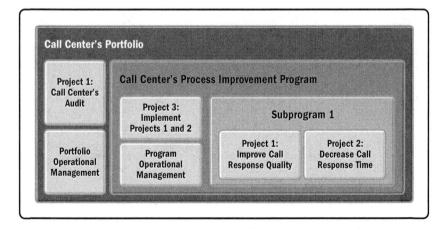

Figure 2-6: Relationship between program, project, and portfolio.

Table 2-3:   Portfolio, program, and project manager roles and responsibilities, detailed comparison.

	Portfolio Manager	Program Manager	Project Manager
Role	Manage a portfolio.	Manage a program.	Manage a project.
Responsibilities	Manage multiple program and project interdependencies.	Manage multiple project interdependencies.	Manage a project.
Execute	Execute coordinated management of portfolio components.	Execute centralized coordinated management of program components.	Execute a project.
Focus	Focus on selecting the right programs and projects, prioritizing work, and providing resources. Focus on resource-leveling with the objective of maximizing the economic use of resources within the portfolio.	Focus on aligning program goals with long-term goals of the organization. Focus on people, politics, and negotiation.	Focus on scope, schedules, and resources. Focus on content.
Leadership Style	Leadership style focuses on adding value to portfolio decision making.	Leadership style focuses on managing relationships and resolving conflicts.	Leadership style focuses on executing tasks and meeting the success criteria.
Provide	Provide insight and synthesis. "Doing the right work" rather than "doing the work right."	Provide vision and manage political aspects of stakeholder management.	Team player who motivates using his or her knowledge and skills.
Monitor	Identify, select, prioritize, govern, monitor, and report contributions of the portfolio components that include programs, subprograms, and projects.	Monitor projects and ongoing work through governance structure.	Monitor and coordinate tasks and the work of producing the project's product(s).
Staff	Manage and coordinate portfolio management staff.	Manage project managers.	Manage technicians, specialists.
Responsibilities	Create and maintain necessary process and communication about the aggregate portfolio.	Ensure alignment of multiple projects with program goals; optimize and integrate cost, schedule, and effort.	Conduct detailed planning to manage the delivery of products of the project.
Measure	Monitor aggregate performance and value indicators.	Maximize return on investment (ROI) and value delivery.	Complete project on time and within budget.
Financial Management	Responsible for achieving financial objectives, frequently with indirect accountability for shareholder value.	Responsible for delivering program benefits on budget.	Responsible for executing the project on budget.

A program manager role includes setting up the program structure, overseeing program execution, monitoring risks, and carrying program profit and loss responsibilities. A project manager role includes managing projects and carrying responsibility for project execution on time and on budget. A portfolio manager role includes identifying, prioritizing, authorizing, managing, and controlling projects, programs, and other related work to achieve specific strategic business objectives.

Using portfolio, program, and project structure and the relationship between them, we can compare the roles of portfolio, programs, and project managers, as presented in Table 2-3.

Portfolio, program, and project manager roles are distinctly different, as evident from the analysis presented in Table 2-1. A portfolio manager focuses on selecting the right programs and projects, prioritizing work, and leveling resources with an objective of maximizing the economic use of resources within the portfolio. A program manager ensures alignment of multiple projects with program goals, and integration of cost, schedule, and effort. A project manager focuses on project scope, schedules, resources, and risk management.

A program manager closely works with the portfolio manager on project prioritization, resource acquisition, and risk escalation. A program manager also receives guidance from a portfolio manager on program structure, resources, and execution. Portfolio and program managers work closely together on portfolio and program process improvement efforts.

A program manager guides project managers on project execution, delivery on time and on budget, project quality, and risk escalation. Program and project managers work closely on process improvement initiatives to improve project execution mechanisms, tools to monitor project progress, and quality checks for project deliverables.

CHAPTER 3

Program Strategy Alignment

This chapter provides an in-depth analysis of the program strategy alignment domain. It describes the criticality of program alignment with the organizational strategy and the elements that a program manager and a program sponsor create to ensure program strategy alignment throughout the program life cycle. These elements include program business case, road map, environmental analysis, and phase-gate review.

During the definition phase, to ensure initial program alignment with the organizational strategy, a program manager creates a business case and a road map. The program manager also conducts an environmental analysis, the results of which become an input to the business case and a road map. During the benefits delivery phase, a program manager conducts phase-gate reviews to ensure the program's continued alignment with the organizational strategy.

This chapter covers the following key aspects:

- Organizational strategy and program alignment;
- Business case;
- Road map;
- Environmental analysis; and
- Phase-gate review.

Organizational Strategy and Program Alignment

A key difference between program and project management is the strategic focus of programs. Programs are designed to align with organizational strategy and ensure organizational benefits are realized.[1] It's not enough for projects and programs to come in on time and on budget. They must also be in sync with strategy, or "it's just wasted capital."[2]

Organizations build strategies to define how the vision will be achieved. Every year, organizations go through an *annual strategic planning cycle*, where organizational vision and mission are translated into a strategic plan within the boundaries of the organizational values. The *strategic plan* consists of initiatives that are influenced in part by market dynamics, customer and partner requests, shareholders, government regulations, and competitor plans and actions. Initiatives may be grouped into portfolios to be executed during a defined period. Portfolios also consist of programs and projects that execute the strategic plan, realizing identified benefits, and, subsequently, execute organizational strategy.

The goal of linking portfolio management with organizational strategy is to establish a balanced, operational plan that will help the organization achieve its goals and balance the use of resources to maximize value in executing programs, projects, and operational activities. The strategic planning and portfolio management processes identify and measure benefits for the organization. They provide programs with a definition of the expected outcomes and results. Organizations initiate programs to deliver benefits and accomplish agreed-upon outcomes that often affect the entire organization. During the program initiation phase, organizations conduct feasibility studies to clarify and define program objectives, requirements, and risks to ensure a program's alignment with the vision, mission, organizational strategy, and objectives.[3]

It has been observed that some organizations do not follow through on the strategic plan execution. Frequently, the strategic plan does not fully cascade down to the program level, creating a gap between strategy formulation and strategy execution. Sometimes, organizations do

---

[1] PMI. (2013). *The standard for program management* – Third edition. Newtown Square, PA: Author.

[2] PMI. (2014). *The project management office: Aligning strategy & implementation*. Newtown Square, PA: Author. Retrieved from http://www.pmi.org/-/media/pmi/documents/public/pdf/white-papers/pmo-strategy-implement.pdf

[3] PMI. (2013). *The standard for program management* – Third edition. Newtown Square, PA: Author.

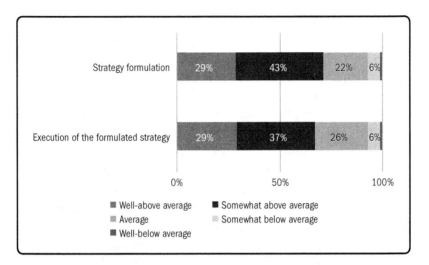

Figure 3-1: Strategy execution.

not establish quantitative and qualitative measures to evaluate execution of the strategic plan and quality of the realized benefits. And, at times, upon program completion, organizations fail to align ongoing operations with implemented changes and incorporate benefits realized through the program execution to the ongoing operations.

Statistical evidence shows that an alarmingly small percentage of organizations execute formulated strategy well-above and somewhat above average compared to peer companies, as shown in Figure 3-1.

Only 39% of organizations consider prioritization and funding of the appropriate strategic initiatives and projects to be essential, 48% of organizations consider prioritization and funding of the appropriate strategic initiatives and projects to be very important, and the remaining 13% consider prioritization and funding of the appropriate strategic initiatives and projects to be somewhat important. Only 56% of organizations find successful project execution essential for strategic results delivery, and 34% and 10% of organizations find successful project execution to be very important and somewhat important for strategic results delivery.[4] Even though this statistic was determined based on the

---

[4] PMI. (2016). *Pulse of the profession®: The high cost of low performance—How will you improve business results?* Newtown Square, PA: Author.

analysis of the project management industry, we will assume that, to a large degree, it also represents the program management industry.

By supporting strategic program implementation, the program management office plays a crucial role in the delivery of the organizational strategy. Organizations that have project management offices with broader business-wide responsibilities, such as an enterprise program management office (EPMO), are closest to the delivery of the strategic value. With the responsibility for aligning projects and programs to corporate strategy, the EPMO establishes and oversees the appropriate governance of enterprise portfolios, programs, and projects; and performs portfolio management functions to ensure strategy alignment and benefits realization.

Effective executive sponsorship is critical to the success of organizational strategy initiatives—an executive sponsor's active engagement is the top driver of project and program success. Data show that, out of all projects with executive sponsors, 76% of projects meet goals or intent. And data show that, out of all projects that do not have executive sponsors, only 46% of projects meet goals or intent. Despite this finding, only three in five projects have engaged executive sponsors. Effective executive sponsors have a thorough knowledge of a project and how it connects to business strategy. And owing to their position and experience, they have the necessary skills and authority to clear roadblocks, the confidence to make quick and effective decisions, and the influence to champion the project with senior management and position it as a top priority. The best executive sponsors can also motivate and engage a project team.[5]

To fully realize program benefits, it is critical to ensure program alignment with the organization's long-term goals and strategy. Alignment refers to the degree to which a program mirrors and supports the priorities of the organization's business strategy. Additionally, it is the degree to which the business strategy is used to guide objectives and work outcomes of the execution team.[6]

Program strategy alignment is achieved through the program vision and program selection process. The program vision is the keystone element that establishes the end state that defines success for the program

---

[5] PMI (2016). *Pulse of the profession®: The high cost of low performance—How will you improve business results?* Newtown Square, PA: Author.

[6] Martinelli, R. J., Waddell, J. M., & Rahschulte, T. J. (2014). *Program management for improved business results.* (2nd ed.). Hoboken, NJ: John Wiley & Sons, Inc.

and provides guidelines for what to do and how to do it. It is rare that the successful execution of a single program results in the attainment of all strategic goals. Rather, it takes the successful execution of some programs within the portfolio. Each program then carries a set of program objectives that are designed to achieve specific strategic goals. The program objectives provide the translation from strategic business goals to actionable execution objectives specific to a program.[7]

We will illustrate how organizational strategy translates into program objectives by using the call center's process improvement program example. An organization has a strategic goal of providing the highest call response quality and fastest call response time. This strategic goal translates into the call center's process improvement program objectives:

- Improve call response quality; and
- Decrease call response time.

We discussed how program strategy alignment is achieved through a program vision. And now, we will discuss how program strategy alignment is achieved through the program selection process. The program selection process depends on where the organization operates along the program management continuum, in the project-oriented or program-oriented space. Project-oriented organizations may have a limited process of selecting programs that are aligned with organizational strategy. Frequently, project-oriented organizations limit their program selection to the programs that permit execution of tactical initiatives.

Program-oriented organizations are likely to have a formalized program selection process that starts with formulating an organizational strategy. During strategy formulation, the organization defines strategy and determines how and during what period it will be executed. An outcome of this work is the strategic plan, a document that outlines organizational strategy and its execution. Once the organizational strategy is formulated, an executive steering committee selects programs, the execution of which will allow the organization to execute strategy. Once programs are selected, the organization commits resources and starts the program definition phase. The program definition phase confirms if

---

[7] Martinelli, R. J., Waddell, J. M., & Rahschulte, T. J. (2014). *Program management for improved business results*. (2nd ed.). Hoboken, NJ: John Wiley & Sons, Inc.

identified programs are the most appropriate to execute organizational strategy and realize program benefits.

The definition phase begins with confirming the need for a program and identifying benefits that a program will realize, both of which are summarized in the business case. A program road map translates the business case into a valuable program execution tool that chronologically represents the program's intended direction. Environmental analysis is conducted to provide an input to the business case and a road map to ensure that a program will deliver expected benefits within the environment where it operates. All of these elements become inputs to a program management plan that establishes an outline for executing organizational strategy and realizing program benefits through the program life cycle. The program management plan will be discussed in detail in Chapter 8: Program Management Infrastructure.

Business Case

The business case is developed during the definition phase. The business case is developed to assess the program balance between costs and benefits. The business case is a document written for executive decision makers, assessing the present and future business value and risks related to a current investment opportunity.[8] A good business case brings confidence and accountability into making investment decisions. The business case is a compilation of information collected during the enterprise analysis and business case processes. The business case is created to help the executive sponsor and stakeholders ensure that a program has value and relative priority compared to alternative programs, based on the objectives and expected benefits laid out in the business case.

In program-oriented organizations, a program manager leads business case preparation. The program manager also collaborates with key sponsors to develop the program business case. The business case can be brief or comprehensive, depending on the organizational structure, and where it operates—in the project-oriented or program-oriented space. The comprehensive business case likely includes program background, benefits, costs, a gap analysis, and known risks.

---

[8] Larson, R., & Larson, E. (2011). *Creating bulletproof business cases*. Minneapolis, MN: Watermark Learning.

The purpose of the program business case is to demonstrate that a program supports the strategic goals of the organization and is used to determine if the organization should invest the financial, human, and capital resources to execute the program fully. Portions of the business case are vital in establishing the program vision by describing the business opportunity available and how the program will achieve the opportunity and business strategy. The business case connects the organizational strategy and objectives to the program objectives and helps identify the level of investment and support required to achieve the program benefits.

The program business case spells out the business benefits of the program and the rationale as to why users, customers, or the organizations desire the program outcome, and why it is better than other alternatives. Most importantly, the business case demonstrates that program benefits will exceed program costs over time. The business case is core to the establishment and execution of the program vision because it is the means of securing the funding and resources necessary to execute the program and for continually evaluating the progress of the program toward achieving the strategic business goals intended.[9]

The business case may be documented in many ways. However, there is a structural framework of the kinds of information that should be included in the business case. At the same time, as every program is different, a comprehensive and convincing business case needs to address a program in context. That may require adding new sections to the structural framework or regrouping material as necessary to address the specifics of a program and the organizational environment it operates in.

The comprehensive business case likely has a framework that includes an executive summary, program strategy alignment, program scope, return on investment (ROI), assumptions, benefits, risk analysis, estimated time line, estimated costs, program team structure, program team roster, supporting subject matter experts, recommendations, and appendices.

An executive summary introduces and describes a program, its benefits, the ROI, and estimated timing to execute it. In simple terms, the executive summary describes what a program is about, how much it will cost, and what benefits it will deliver and when.

---

[9] Martinelli, R. J., Waddell, J. M., & Rahschulte, T. J. (2014). *Program management for improved business results.* (2nd ed.). Hoboken, NJ: John Wiley & Sons, Inc.

Using the strategic plan as an input, the program strategy alignment section describes how the program will execute organizational strategy.

The program scope section defines general program scope. Detailed program scope is defined in the program management plan during the program benefits delivery phase when all program information is known.

The return on investment (ROI) section calculates profit gained after program execution is weighed against program costs. The calculation may show short-term and long-term ROI as well as ROI each year during a defined period.

The assumptions section includes a list of assumptions that must hold true for a program execution to be successful. Each assumption includes an impact that describes what would happen to a program execution if the assumption does not hold true (e.g., it may result in execution delay or in cost increase).

The benefits section, in quantifiable terms, defines program benefits that will be realized after program execution.

The risk analysis section lists all known risks that can impact program execution. Each risk includes a description, the probability of occurrence, mitigation strategy, persons responsible for risk mitigation, target resolution date, and risk impact on the program, categorized as high, medium, or low.

The estimated time line section describes all phases of the program life cycle. Each phase has scheduled start and finish dates. And, each phase includes key deliverables and milestones, along with corresponding dates.

The estimated costs section itemizes program costs for the entire program life cycle, broken down by program phases. Costs may also be broken into various categories (e.g., operational and capital).

The program team structure section describes team member roles, and it documents relationships among program team members using an organizational chart.

The program team roster lists the candidates for each role on the program team. It includes names, titles, skills, and percent allocation to the program.

The supporting subject matter experts section lists individuals who will not be members of a program team, but will provide subject matter expertise when needed. The list includes roles, names, positions, and descriptions of the subject matter expertise.

The recommendation section includes a recommendation for program approval or denial, and outlines reasons for a recommendation. The reasoning is substantiated by the findings discussed in the preceding sections of the business case.

Appendices may include supporting data, research reports, associated documents, and other supporting materials.

Once the program business case is completed, the program manager reviews the business case with the executive sponsor and stakeholders and gains their approvals. Once approved, the business case establishes the authority, intent, and philosophy of the business need. The business case also serves as a formal declaration of the value that the program is expected to deliver, and a justification for the resources that will be expended to deliver it. The business case is a key input for organizational leadership to charter and authorize programs.[10]

One of the top issues we hear from our training clients is that projects often get justified or initiated by the solution. The issue results from a project either not having a business case or having a business case with insufficient content. The resulting solution then often doesn't completely solve the underlying problem: rework then results; and the ongoing pain the project was intended to address will continue.

Inadequate or nonexistent business cases usually result in unclear project scope, often leading to scope creep, which results in rework, cost overruns, and delays. Also, inappropriate approaches on projects often lead to rigid solutions, such as selecting a commercial-off-the-shelf (COTS) package when a custom solution is warranted. Missing or ineffective business cases also tend to cause numerous changes and time and cost overruns, because the product requirements are often not clear up front.[11]

As the business case is sometimes mistaken with the statement of work (SOW), it is important to outline how the two documents differ from one another. A statement of work and a business case serve different purposes and, therefore, contain different information. A *statement of work* (SOW) is a document routinely employed in the field of project management. It defines project-specific activities, deliverables, and time lines for a vendor providing services to the client.[12]

---

[10] PMI. (2013). *The standard for program management* – Third edition. Newtown Square, PA: Author.

[11] Larson, R., & Larson, E. (2011). *Creating bulletproof business cases.* Minneapolis, MN: Watermark Learning.

[12] Statement of work. (n.d.). In *Wikipedia.* Retrieved from https://en.wikipedia.org/wiki/Statement_of_work

A statement of work outlines products and services that will be provided by projects. It is a document that is created for external use. The business case confirms the business need and justifies funding for the project by providing cost-benefit analysis. It is created for internal use.

Road Map

The *program road map* should be both a chronological representation in a graphical form of a program's intended direction as well as a set of documented success criteria for each of the chronological events. It depicts key dependencies between major milestones, communicates the linkage between the business strategy and the planned prioritized work, reveals and explains gaps, and provides a high-level view of key milestones and decision points. The road map also summarizes key end-point objectives, challenges, and risks, and provides a high-level snapshot of the supporting infrastructure and component plans.

The program road map can be a valuable tool for managing the execution of the program and for assessing the program's progress toward achieving its expected benefits. To enable effective program governance, the program road map can be used to show how components are organized into major stages or blocks; however, it does not include the internal details of the specific components.[13]

The business case provides input to the road map. A program manager may use the road map template developed within the organization or may build a road map using software packages like PowerPoint, Excel, or Microsoft Project. Excel and Microsoft Project have free road map standardized templates.

To illustrate how to build a road map, we will use the call center's process improvement program example. As was described earlier, the program includes subprogram one that includes project one—improve call response quality—and project two—decrease call response time. The program also includes project three—implement projects one and

---

[13] PMI. (2013). *The standard for program management* – Third edition. Newtown Square, PA: Author.

two in all call centers. During the program definition phase, the following program and component information is available:

- The program is scheduled to start on 3 October 2016.
- Phase 1 of the program includes executing project one. Project one is scheduled to start on 3 October 2016. It has a duration of three months, and project one will deliver benefits on 30 December 2016.
- Phase 2 of the program includes executing project two. Project two is scheduled to start on 2 January 2017. It has a duration of three months, and project two will deliver benefits on 31 March 2017.
- Phase 3 of the program includes executing project three. It is scheduled to start on 3 April 2017. It has a duration of six months, and project three will implement projects one and two in all call centers on 29 September 2017.
- The program is scheduled to end on 29 September 2017.

Using the information outlined above, a program manager built the call center's process improvement program road map in Excel, as shown in Figure 3-2.

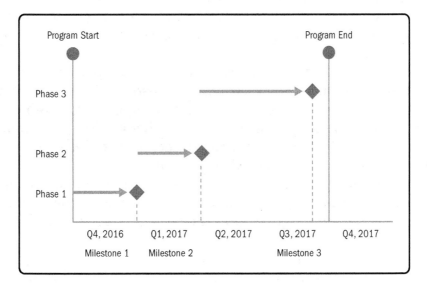

Figure 3-2:   The call center's process improvement program road map.

After program approval, the road map becomes one of the key inputs to the program management plan; the first draft of which is built during the program definition phase, as will be described in Chapter 8: Program Management Infrastructure.

Environmental Analysis

Internal and external factors influence any program, impacting program execution success. Internal factors are factors that exist within the organization but outside the program. Organizational structure is an example of an internal factor that impacts a program. Whether an organization is project-oriented or program-oriented defines many aspects of program execution, including program structure and the program manager role. Examples of internal factors include corporate culture, funding, and resource availability. External factors are factors that exist outside the organization. Examples of external factors include regulatory requirements, political instability, and natural disasters.

Environmental analysis is a process of identifying internal and external factors, analyzing their impact on a program, and developing a plan to mitigate risks that internal and external factors present to the program. There are many types of environmental analyses, including comparative advantage analysis; feasibility studies; assumptions analysis; historical information; and strengths, weaknesses, opportunities, and threats (SWOT) analysis.

Comparative advantage analysis is a comparison of a program with real or hypothetical programs. The analysis uses the business case as a main source of information. The analysis takes into consideration that a program may have competing efforts that either reside within an organization or are external to it. It also includes a what-if analysis of how program benefits may be realized by other means.

Feasibility studies analyze the feasibility of a program within an organization, including funding and resource availability, complexity, and constraints. A feasibility study uses the business case as a main source of information.

Assumptions analysis is a process of identifying and documenting program assumptions. It is an iterative process performed throughout the program life cycle. Initially, program assumptions are identified during the definition phase, and they are validated during the benefits delivery phase to ensure that the assumptions have not been annulled by new information and program activities.

Historical information analysis identifies success factors and reasons for the failure of the programs that the organization completed in the past. Historical information analysis uses all artifacts from the previously completed programs, including business cases, road maps, environmental analyses, risks logs, and program management plans. Historical information analysis becomes a source of lessons learned from the previously completed programs and best practices for the future programs.

SWOT is an analysis of the strengths, weaknesses, opportunities, and threats of the program. This analysis helps identify program risks and provides information for the program charter and program management plan.

Phase-Gate Review

It is important to choose the right program that will allow executing organizational strategy. However, it is equally important to continue to ensure program alignment with the organizational strategy throughout the program life cycle. Elements that ensure program alignment during the definition phase are a business case, road map, and environmental analysis, as was discussed in the preceding sections. Elements that ensure program alignment during the benefits delivery phase are phase-gate and readiness reviews.

Phase gate is a review at the end of a phase in which a decision is made to either continue to the next phase, continue with modification, or end a project or program.[14] Phase-gate review is conducted at the end of each phase of the program. The review uses multiple criteria, including continued assurance of the program alignment with organization strategy. Phase-gate review criteria include:

- Business rationale that confirms the program continued business need and the organization's strategy alignment;
- Quality of execution that confirms quality of benefits; and
- An action plan that confirms timing and resources needed to continue program execution.

---

[14] PMI. (2015). *PMI lexicon of project management terms, Version 3.0.* Newtown Square, PA: Author.

CHAPTER 4

Program Benefits /solutions Realization and Management

Benefits realization is one of the main reasons organizations employ programs. This chapter provides an in-depth analysis of the program benefits realization domain. It defines business value, and business results are helping us understand the differences between the two. Analyzing the program management continuum shows how benefits delivery increases as the organization moves into the program-oriented space. This chapter describes that benefits management is achieved by employing the benefits management strategy, which includes five phases: benefits identification, benefits analysis and planning, benefits delivery, benefits transition, and benefits sustainment.

The chapter includes the following sections:

- Benefits realization; and
- Benefits management.

Benefits Realization

One of the main reasons organizations deploy programs is to realize benefits. Focusing on the business value for the client has helped many teams select the best solution for each project, facilitate decision making on product construction methods, and prioritize projects within the program.[1] Before analyzing how a program manages benefits realization, it is important to define a benefit and examine benefit components.

A *benefit* is an outcome of actions and behaviors that provides utility, value, or a positive change to the intended recipient.[2] Programs realize various types of benefits, including the development of new products and services, entrance into new markets, growth of the market share, improvement of financial organizational results, improvement of organizational processes, and more. Program benefits are comprised of two components: business value and business results.

Business Value

Business value encompasses the synergistic improvements that program management can provide to optimize the business functions of the enterprise. For example, the key business value that any program provides to the organization is a benefit realized from managing related projects as a program. For example, the key business value generated by the call center's process improvement program is an integrated implementation of projects one and two in all call centers. Additional examples of program business value include achieving business scalability through the assumption of business management responsibilities at the program level, integrating business functional elements for deployment effort, and aligning financial objects with the business objects.

Organizations realize program business value by optimizing some business functions:

- Aligning business strategy and execution;
- Integrating business functions;
- Navigating business and environmental ambiguity;
- Achieving business scalability;
- Managing distributed collaboration; and
- Reducing time-to-benefit.

---

[1] Merrick, A. (2015). *Allied forces*. Retrieved from http://www.pmi.org/-/media/pmi/landing-pages/business-analysis-tools-silverpop/pdf/allied-forces-project-management-business-analysis.pdf

[2] PMI. (2013). *The standard for program management* – Third edition. Newtown Square, PA: Author.

Aligning Business Strategy and Execution

For many organizations, program management provides value by ensuring program alignment with the organizational strategy. Program management creates a critical linkage between strategic goals, program objectives, and program benefits. Initially, the linkage is being established during the program definition phase while preparing the program business case. The linkage is confirmed during the benefits delivery phase by conducting phase-gate reviews.

Integrating Business Functions

Program management adds business value by serving as a mechanism that integrates works of various operating functions within the organization to create an effective business model. Program management integrates collective efforts by focusing various functions on a common purpose, an achievement of improved business results.

Navigating Business and Environmental Ambiguity

By employing program management principles to business and environmental ambiguity, an organization will realize the following key benefits:

- Provide the leadership necessary to coalesce multiple perspectives and agendas effectively;
- Develop a framework to enable flexible management of change; and
- Appoint a business champion to ensure that the strategic goals set forth by senior management are achieved.

Achieving Business Scalability

Program management offers business value by providing an organization with a pathway to effectively scale business by assuming management of ROI duties for the development of each new capability.

Managing Distributed Collaboration

Effectiveness requires an integration of work efforts to satisfy growing complexity. However, another modern phenomenon, distributed teams, has added a layer of complexity to the integration of multiple work outcomes. Many companies have historically operated under a traditional structure, characterized by strongly siloed departments or groups, where horizontal collaboration across these departments was difficult, let alone collaboration across the globe. One by one, these companies are realizing a need to adopt a distributed model to be able to not only compete, but also in many cases, to survive.

Many companies that are succeeding in managing these increasingly distributed environments are doing two key things:

- Adopting a systems approach to developing capabilities; and
- Adopting program management to integrate solutions effectively.

Early adopter companies in the automotive, aerospace, and defense industries continue to utilize this approach. Most recently, companies such as Apple, salesforce.com, Intel, and Kaiser Permanente, among others, have found great success in utilizing systems and platform concepts coupled with program management to develop their new capabilities.

Reducing Time-to-Benefit

Besides demanding increasingly complex solutions, customers also want accelerated delivery of new capabilities. It is a well-known fact that in today's highly competitive world, time-to-benefits is a critical factor in gaining an advantage.

If an organization has a strong program management function, products are closer to what the customers want, and the team spends less time iterating late in the program to meet customer expectations. A program manager adds clarity for the engineering team by balancing market requests with the engineering capabilities, therefore setting realistic customer targets. This results in the most efficient use of resources, which allows a program team to deliver what the customer wants the first time.[3]

Business Results

Business results are tangible business outcomes derived from creating and implementing new products and services, and any other capabilities

---

[3] Martinelli, R. J., Waddell, J. M., Rahschulte, T. J. (2014). *Program management for improved business results*. (2nd ed.). Hoboken, NJ: John Wiley & Sons, Inc.

delivered by the program. Examples of business results include increased profitability, expanded market share, lowered product cost, and increased productivity. The call center's process improvement program achieved two business results: improved call response quality and decreased call response time.

There is a direct correlation between how program management is implemented within an organization and a volume of benefits realized through program management. Analysis of the program management continuum shows that benefits delivery increases as the organization moves to the right into the program-oriented space, as shown in Figure 2-2. The shift to the program-oriented organization allows for strengthening program strategy alignment and increasing benefits delivery.

Project-oriented organizations utilize programs that are formed from the combination of pre-existing projects and other work activities into a single entity. In this program type, a realization occurs that the projects may be more effectively managed under a single program. This realization is driven by a desire on the part of an organization's execution team to make a more strategic approach to work that gets accomplished within their organization.

In program-oriented organizations, by contrast, programs are most often driven by the strategic goals of an organization. Strategic objectives define strategic programs, and, therefore, define business results desired from the creation delivery of the program output.

As business makes a conscious decision to become more program-oriented, the responsibility for delivering business results begins to fall upon the program manager.[4] In program-oriented organizations, a program manager becomes increasingly accountable for realizing benefits. A program manager ensures that business benefits are obtained by delivering an integrated solution, providing program leadership, coordinating multiple projects within a program, and collaborating with multiple business functions within the organization. A program manager can accomplish this through effective benefits management, as was described in detail in Chapter 2: What Makes a Successful Program Manager?

---

[4] Martinelli, R. J., Waddell, J. M., & Rahschulte, T. J. (2014). *Program management for improved business results*. (2nd ed.). Hoboken, NJ: John Wiley & Sons, Inc.

Benefits realization illustrates and measures how projects and programs add true value to the enterprise. Benefits realization is challenging, but when executed right, it helps ensure that the outcome of a project produces desired benefits. This is achieved by establishing, measuring, and communicating organizational initiatives results. Such insight into performance is an essential planning tool for future projects.

Organizations with mature benefits realization processes benefit from:

- Clearly identified strategic rewards;
- Effectively assessed and monitored risks;
- Proactively planned necessary organizational changes;
- Explicitly defined accountability for project success; and
- Routinely extended responsibility for project team integration.

Organizations that implement benefits realization programs understand this value because they are capturing the hard facts needed to showcase the return on their project management investments. Nevertheless, far too few organizations have effective benefits realization programs in place. In fact, many have no benefits realization program at all, so they are missing an opportunity to understand what would help them increase the rate of project success. We need to continue studying the challenges of benefits realization to gain insight into ways organizations can meet those challenges.

Pulse of the Profession®: Capturing the Value of Project Management (2015), published by the Project Management Institute, indicates that only one in five organizations report having a high level of benefits realization maturity. While low, this still represents an increase of 63% since 2013, indicating a high level of interest in this topic, even while organizations struggle to become adept at it. High performers are over four times more likely to report high benefits realization maturity, 39% compared to 9% of low performers, because they recognize it as a business imperative.

Also, organizations that report high benefits realization maturity have significantly better project outcomes, as noted in Figure 4-1.[5]

---

[5] PMI. (2015). *Pulse of the profession®: Capturing the value of project management.* Newtown Square, PA: Author.

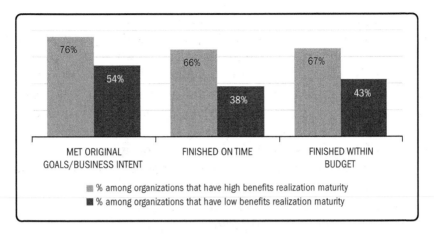

Figure 4-1:   Benefits realization and project outcomes.

To successfully realize program benefits, it is important to develop an approach and tools to measure program benefits, as will be discussed in the next section.

Benefits Management

Benefits management can be achieved by using a *program benefits management strategy* that defines how a program will contribute to the realization of organizational strategic goals, if the program receives necessary funds and is properly executed. A program benefits management strategy is used to guide program execution by keeping a program aligned with the business results.

Program benefits management strategy development occurs during the program definition phase. During this phase, the program manager identifies, defines, and qualifies benefits. The program benefits management strategy is used to guide program execution as it keeps the program aligned to the business results desired.

One of the common issues that a program manager may encounter during the program benefits delivery phase is misalignment between intended business goals and a program output. To mitigate this issue, a program manager can use a benefits mapping tool to check and ensure that all components of a program are aligned with the benefits management strategy.

Program benefits management is a process of identifying a program's planned benefits and monitoring the program's ability to realize them. The purpose of program benefits management is to focus program stakeholders on the outcomes and benefits to be provided by the various activities conducted throughout the program. To do that, a program manager employs program benefits management to continually:

- Identify and assess value and impact of program benefits;
- Align expected benefits with the organization's goals and objectives;
- Assign responsibility and accountability for the realization of benefits provided by the program;
- Monitor interdependencies between outputs delivered by projects within a program, and ensure that these outputs contribute to the program benefits;
- Analyze potential impact of planned program changes on the expected benefits delivery; and
- Ensure that realized program benefits could be sustained.

During the program benefits delivery phase, program components are planned, developed, integrated, and managed to facilitate delivery of the intended program benefits. During the program benefits delivery phase, the benefits analysis and planning activities, along with the benefits delivery activities, may be performed in an interactive fashion, especially if corrective actions are required to achieve program benefits.

Program benefits management requires continuous interaction with other performance domains throughout the program life cycle. Interactions are cyclical in nature and begin top-down during the program definition phase and bottom-up during the program benefits delivery phase. For example, program strategy alignment, in conjunction with program stakeholder engagement, provides the critical inputs/parameters to the program, including vision, mission, strategic goals and objectives, and the preliminary business case that defines the program benefits. Program performance data are evaluated through program governance to ensure that the program will produce its intended benefits and outcomes.

Program benefits management takes place throughout the entire program life cycle and includes benefits identification, benefits analysis

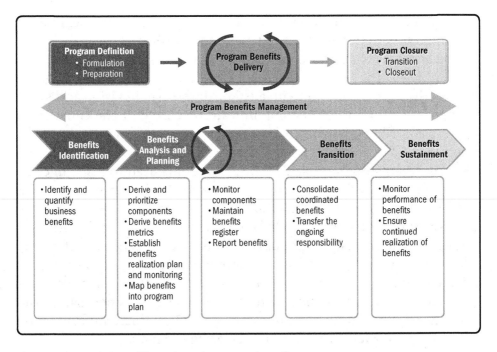

Figure 4-2:   Program life cycle and program benefits management.

and planning, benefits delivery, benefits transition, and benefits sustainment, as shown in the Figure 4-2.[6]

Benefits Identification

Benefits identification occurs early on during the program life cycle, during the formulation subphase of the definition phase. During benefits identification, a program manager analyzes available elements, including program business case, a road map, environmental analysis, and other relevant information to identify and quantify benefits. The analysis includes deriving and prioritizing benefits components. It also includes preparing a metric that will allow measuring benefits during

---

[6] Merrick, A. (2015). *Allied forces*. Retrieved from http://www.pmi.org/-/media/pmi/landing-pages/business-analysis-tools-silverpop/pdf/allied-forces-project-management-business-analysis.pdf

the program execution phase. After identifying benefits, the next step is mapping them to the project outcomes and deliverables.

The *benefits map* provides traceability between project outcomes and deliverables to the benefits intended from the output of the program. This is critical information to first establish the overall vision and scope for a program, and then to communicate how each of the constituent projects contributes to the goals of a program, and finally to trace the execution of the program and projects to final delivery of business benefits. Like many program-based tools, this tool is used to assist in characterizing how specific program objectives are met. However, benefits maps can become complex and confusing due to the one-to-many relationships between project deliverables and outcomes to the program objectives. The critical component in building an effective benefits map is to ensure each project deliverable or outcome is mapped to a program objective, and every objective to the business factors. For more complex programs, it is recommended that the mapping is performed and represented in tablature form to establish order, reduce confusion, and maintain greater value than effort in creating the map.

The benefits map is intended to be used throughout the life of the program to analyze consequences caused by adjustments and changes as they occur to the original program vision and scope. The first use of the benefits map normally occurs as part of the business case development process, where a high-level mapping of benefits to program objectives to strategic intent is established. Further detail is then added during detailed planning when the full comprehension of program scope and traceability of project outcomes to business benefits is necessary.[7]

A program benefits map includes the following data:

- Organizational strategic goals;
- Business success factors that translate an organizational strategic goal to program objectives using various categories (e.g., finance, accounting, marketing, time, quality, etc.);
- Program objectives that group business success factors into categories listed above; and
- Program deliverables that result from the program objectives.

---

[7] Martinelli, R. J., Waddell, J. M., & Rahschulte, T. J. (2014). *Program management for improved business results.* (2nd ed.). Hoboken, NJ: John Wiley & Sons, Inc.

Using the call center's process improvement program example, we will build a program benefits map, which will include the following:

- The organizational strategic goal is to provide the highest call response quality and the fastest call response time;
- Business success factors translate the strategic organizational goal into two categories: quality and time;
- Program objectives for quality and time are:
  - Quality objective is to improve call response quality by 25%;
  - Time objective is to decrease call response time by 30 seconds;
- Program deliverables for quality and time are:
  - Quality deliverable is to improve call response scripts;
  - Time deliverable is to improve call response workflows.

Along with the program work breakdown structure and the program architecture, the benefits map is a useful tool for establishing the overall scope of a program and for demonstrating the alignment between project outcomes and deliverables to the objectives of a program. The benefits map can also be used to communicate to senior leadership, the overall program team, and other program stakeholders how the strategy of the organization and program are melded together, and how each program benefit will be realized.

There are several advantages to be gained by both senior management of an organization and the program team through the use of the benefits map. It helps to create better clarification and understanding of the program vision and scope, and establishes direct alignment between program objectives, project outcomes, and the business benefits to be realized. The benefits map also provides a systematic process for assessing program benefits as part of the program's cost-benefit analysis, which is a critical element of the business case for a program. Finally, it enables focused tracking and monitoring of progress toward realization of the benefits as part of the program governance process, and establishes an effective means of evaluating the success of a program from a benefits realization perspective.[8]

---

[8] Martinelli, R. J., Waddell, J. M., & Rahschulte, T. J. (2014). *Program management for improved business results* (2nd ed.). Hoboken, NJ: John Wiley & Sons, Inc.

After benefits are identified and mapped, to ensure full realization, it is important to track benefits. Benefits tracking involves examining program progress toward benefits realization. If the critical business success factors are defined and consistently reviewed as a part of the program governance system, the means to objectively evaluate the value of the program is available to the program sponsor and the governance board.

A tool that assists with benefits tracking is called a benefits register. The *benefits register* collects and lists the planned benefits for the program and is used to measure and communicate the delivery of benefits throughout the duration of the program.[9] Depending on the complexity of the program, the register may include the following fields:

aka solutions tracker in agile

- Benefit item number;
- Benefit name;
- Benefit description;
- How benefit will be realized;
- Benefit mapping to a component;
- Benefit measurement;
- Person responsible for benefits delivery;
- Benefit realization date; and
- Status, including not started, in progress, and complete.

It is important to note that the benefits register is updated iteratively during the benefits delivery phase, as not all component information may be known during the definition phase. We will use the call center's process improvement program to prepare a benefits register. The register lists two benefits: improve call response quality by 25% and decrease call response time by 30 seconds, as shown in Table 4-1.

Benefits Analysis and Planning

Benefits analysis and planning institutes how benefits are realized, and establishes how benefits realization is monitored by developing benefits metrics. Benefits metrics are critical to the successful realization

---

[9] PMI. (2013). *The standard for program management* – Third edition. Newtown Square, PA: Author.

Table 4-1:   Benefits register for the call center's process improvement program.

#	Benefit Name	Description	How Benefit Will be Realized	Benefit Mapping to a Component	Benefit Measurement	Person Responsible	Realization Date	Status
1	Improve call response quality	Improve call response quality by 25%	Improve call response scripts	Project one	Conduct customer survey before and after implementation to confirm quality increase of 25%	Project manager one	12/30/2016	Open
2	Decrease call response time	Decrease call response time by 30 seconds	Improve call response workflows	Project two	Analyze call response time statistics before and after implementation to confirm response time decrease of 30 seconds	Project manager two	3/31/2017	Open

of benefits, as it allows for monitoring incremental benefits delivery. *Benefits metrics* should include incremental benefits delivery dates and quantifiable benefits delivery measures. Quantifiable benefits delivery measures may include percentage completed by a certain date, percentage improved quality, time saved or reduced, percent increased market share, and percentage completed product design or readiness. Incremental and full benefits realization is tracked in the benefits register during the entire program life cycle.

We will use the call center's process improvement program to illustrate benefits metrics. The program has three benefits, each of which has incremental benefits realization metrics. For example, incremental metrics for improving call response quality is a percent improvement for call scripts. Incremental metrics for decreasing call response time is a percent improvement of call response workflows. Incremental metrics for implementing projects one and two in the call centers is some call centers with completed implementation.

The program manager builds a *benefits realization plan* that formally documents the activities necessary for achieving the program's planned benefits. It defines how and when benefits are expected to be delivered to the organization and specifies mechanisms that should be in place to ensure that the benefits are fully realized over time. The benefits realization plan is the baseline document that guides the delivery of benefits during the program's performance. The benefits realization plan also identifies the associated activities, processes, and systems needed for a change driven by the realization of benefits; the required changes to existing processes and systems; and how and when the transition to an operational state will occur.[10]

Utilizing the benefits realization plan, a program manager builds a program road map, a chronological representation that depicts key dependencies between major milestones, communicates linkage between the business strategy and the planned, prioritized work, reveals and explains the gaps, and provides a high-level view of the key milestones and decision points. The program road map summarizes key end-point objectives, challenges, and risks; describes evolving aspects of the program; and provides a high-level snapshot of the supporting infrastructure and components plans.[11] A program manager updates a program road map during the benefits delivery phase, as will be described in the next section.

Benefits Delivery

Benefits delivery ensures that the program delivers benefits as defined in the business case. Organizations deploy programs to realize benefits. Program benefits are expected to exceed program costs over time, as specified in the business case.[12] Benefits management is an iterative process. As all component information becomes available during the program benefits delivery phase, benefits analysis and planning and benefits delivery may be continuously revised with the new information. Revisions translate into changes to many program documents, including the benefits realization plan.

---

[10] PMI. (2013). *The standard for program management* – Third edition. Newtown Square, PA: Author.

[11] PMI. (2013). *The standard for program management* – Third edition. Newtown Square, PA: Author.

[12] PMI. (2013). *The standard for program management* – Third edition. Newtown Square, PA: Author.

A program has multiple components, including subprograms and component projects. Each component is integrated into the program. Start and finish of the components are also milestones for the program as a whole. Completion of the components marks the realization of the component and program benefits.

We will use the call center's process improvement program example. The program includes a subprogram one that includes projects one and two, and project three. Each component has start and finish dates that become program milestones:

- Subprogram one starts on 3 October 2016 with the start of the project one;
- Project one finishes on 30 December 2016 with the delivery of the project one benefit;
- Project two starts on 2 January 2017;
- Project two finishes on 31 March 2017 with the delivery of the project two benefit;
- Project three starts on 3 April 2017;
- Project three finishes on 29 September 2017 with the implementation of projects one and two in all call centers.

For a benefit to have value, it should be realized to a sufficient degree and promptly. The actual benefits delivered by the program components or the program itself should be regularly evaluated against the expected benefits, as defined in the benefits realization plan. A key aspect to consider is whether program component (and even the program as a whole), are still viable. This could occur if the program's value proposition has changed (e.g., if the overall life cycle cost will exceed the proposed benefits, or if the benefits will be delivered too late). Effective governance helps ensure that the promised value is achieved as benefits are delivered. That is why the program governance domain integrates with the benefits management domain to help ensure that the program is continuously aligned with the organizational strategy and that the intended value can still be achieved by the delivery of program benefits:

- Strategy alignment focuses on ensuring the linkage of enterprise and program plans; on defining, maintaining, and validating the program value proposition; and on aligning program management with the enterprise operations management.

- Value delivery focuses on ensuring that the program delivers the promised benefits and that these benefits translate into value.[13]

Benefits Transition

Benefits transition ensures that program benefits are transitioned to operational areas and can be sustained once they are transferred. Value is delivered when the organization, community, or other program beneficiaries can utilize these benefits. Benefits transition ensures that the scope of the transition is defined, the stakeholders in the receiving organizations or function are identified and participate in the planning, the program benefits are measured and sustainment plans are developed, and the transition is executed. Benefits transition planning activities within the program are only one part of the complete transition process. The receiving organization or function is responsible for all preparation processes and activities within their domain to ensure that the product, service, or capability is received and incorporated into their domain.

Benefits may be realized before the formal work of the program has ended and will likely continue long after the formal work has been completed. Benefits transition may be performed following the close of an individual program component if that component is intended to provide incremental benefits to the organization. Benefits transition may also occur following the close of the overall program if the program as a whole is intended to provide benefits to the organization and no incremental benefits have been identified.[14]

We will use the call center's process improvement program example. Even though components have incremental benefits, program benefits are not realized until the program ends. Project one delivers an incremental benefit of improved call response scripts and project two delivers an incremental benefit of improved call response workflows. However, the program benefit of implementing both projects one and two in all call centers is not realized until the program ends.

The program may have different benefits recipients (e.g., internal and external, various departments, and other programs). In the call center's

---

[13] PMI. (2013). *The standard for program management* – Third edition. Newtown Square, PA: Author.
[14] PMI. (2013). *The standard for program management* – Third edition. Newtown Square, PA: Author.

process improvement program, program benefits recipients are all call centers.

Some organizations do not transition benefits to the ongoing operations, resulting in lost benefits, wasted capital, and lost window of opportunities. Key reasons behind deficiency around benefits transition include departments operating in silos and lack of communication during the program execution. Ensuring program benefits transition is vital to the organizational success. To ensure alignment with the transitioning department requires formal benefits transition processes and effective governance.

Benefits Sustainment

Benefits sustainment ensures that ongoing sustainment activities have been transitioned to the appropriate entities or subsequent programs to steward the ongoing post-transition work. As the program is closed, responsibility for sustaining the benefits provided by the program may pass to another organization. Benefits may be sustained through operations, maintenance, new projects and programs, or other efforts. A benefits sustainment plan should be developed before program closure to identify the risks, processes, measures, metrics, and tools necessary to ensure the continued realization of the benefits delivered. Ongoing sustainment of the program benefits should be planned by the program manager and the components project managers during the performance of the program. However, the actual work that ensures the sustainment of benefits is typically conducted after the close of the program and is beyond the scope of the individual component projects.[15]

Currently, it is being observed that some organizations do not sustain benefits during the ongoing operations. It results in rework, additional spending, and duplicate resource usage. Deficiency around benefits sustainment may occur due to lack of accountability for benefits sustainment and an absence of a formal benefits sustainment plan. Ensuring program benefits sustainment is vital to organizational success. To ensure benefits sustainment, it is important to have a formal benefits sustainment plan, and effective governance to ensure accountability of the transitioned department for benefits sustainment.

---

[15] PMI. (2013). *The standard for program management* – Third edition. Newtown Square, PA: Author.

CHAPTER 5

Stakeholder Engagement

As stakeholders have a different level of interest in the program, it is important to manage their expectations based on their needs. This chapter describes the stakeholder engagement domain, including how to engage and manage stakeholders. It introduces a stakeholder map, a tool that allows managing stakeholders. The chapter concludes by describing how to manage conflicting stakeholder priorities.

The chapter covers the following key aspects:

- Stakeholder identification; and
- Stakeholder engagement and conflicting priorities management.

Stakeholder Identification

Since multiple stakeholders will likely have a voice in whether or not a program is funded, stakeholder management is a critical responsibility for the program manager to fulfill. The existence of differing needs, desires, and competing agendas among key stakeholders may never be as high on a program as when the major investment decision is approaching. A program manager should expect to spend significant time engaging with his or her stakeholders. Stakeholder engagement will involve gaining agreement on the program value proposition, gaining the commitment of resources to execute the program, and addressing the concerns of the stakeholders as best possible.[1]

Stakeholders represent all those who will interact with the program as well as those who will be affected by the implementation of the

---

[1] Martinelli, R. J., Waddell, J. M., & Rahschulte, T. J. (2014). *Program management for improved business results.* (2nd ed.). Hoboken, NJ: John Wiley & Sons, Inc.

program. Program and project managers have traditionally classified and managed stakeholder expectations like the approach for identifying and responding to risks. Stakeholders, like risks, should be identified, studied, categorized, and tracked. Stakeholders, like risks, may be internal or external to the program and may have a positive or negative impact on the outcome of the program. Program and project managers need to be aware of both stakeholders and risks to understand and address the changing environments of programs and projects.[2]

Initial program stakeholder identification is performed during the definition phase. The goal during this phase is to identify as many stakeholders as possible. Documents that help identify stakeholders include business case, road map, and environmental analysis. Identified stakeholders are being logged into the stakeholder register. As more information about a program becomes available during the benefits delivery phase, additional stakeholders may be identified and logged into the register. A critical success factor is to create a register early and update it regularly during the benefits delivery phase.

Stakeholder types may vary for different organizations and programs. Examples of program stakeholders include:

- *The program sponsor* is an individual who champions a program, and is responsible for providing program resources and delivering program benefits.
- *The program governance board* is a group responsible for ensuring that program goals are achieved and providing support for addressing program risks across the organization.
- *The program manager* is an individual responsible for managing the program.
- *The project manager* is an individual responsible for managing the component projects within the program.
- *Program team members* are individuals performing program activities.
- *Project team members* are individuals performing constituent project activities.

---

[2] PMI. (2013). *The standard for program management* – Third edition. Newtown Square, PA: Author.

- *The funding organization* is a part of an organization or an external organization providing funding for the program.
- *The performing organization* is a group that is performing the work of the program through component projects and nonproject work.
- *The program management office* is an organization responsible for defining and managing the program-related governance processes, procedures, and templates, supporting individual program management teams by handling administrative functions centrally, or providing dedicated assistance to the program manager.
- *Customers* are individuals or organizations that will use the new capabilities/results of the program and derive the anticipated benefits. The customer is the major stakeholder in the program final result and will influence whether the program is judged to be successful or not.
- *Potential customers* are past and future customers who will be watching intently to see how well the program delivers the stated benefits.
- *Suppliers* are product and service providers who are often affected by changing policies and procedures.
- *Governmental regulatory agencies* are organizations that operate within the regulatory and legal boundaries of their local and national sovereign governments, as well as other related nongovernmental organizations that set standards or requirements that must be adhered to.
- *Competitors* rely on the benefits of the performing organization program as a component of one of their programs. Thus, competitors are interested in the success of the program. Competitors may also benchmark their success in comparison to the performing organization's success. Impacted competitors may be managed as stakeholders.
- *Affected individuals or organizations* are those who perceive that they will either benefit from or be disadvantaged by the program activities.
- *Other groups* are groups representing the consumer, environmental, or other interests.

Stakeholders have a different level of interest in and influence over the program. Having a different level of needs, various stakeholders require a different level of management. A stakeholder map, presented in Figure 5-1, aids with analyzing stakeholders and breaking them into four different categories based on their level of interest in the program:

- *Manage closely* is the category that includes high-power and high-interest stakeholders that have both high interest in and high influence over a program.
- *Keep satisfied* is the category that includes high-power and low-interest stakeholders that have low interest in, but significant influence over a program.
- *Keep informed* is the category that includes low-power and high-interest stakeholders that have high interest in but low influence over a program.
- *Monitor with minimum effort* is the category that includes low-power and low-interest stakeholders that have both low interest in and low influence over a program.

Using the program stakeholder list, we will assign each stakeholder into one of the four categories on the stakeholder map.

- The *manage closely* category includes the program sponsor, the program governance board, the program manager, and a funding organization.

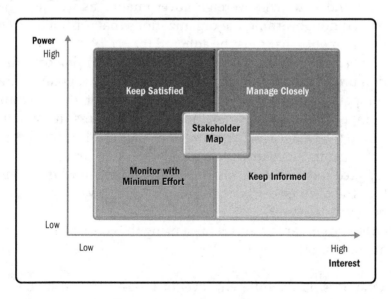

Figure 5-1:   Stakeholder map.

- The *keep satisfied* category includes the program management office, government regulatory agencies, and suppliers.
- The *keep informed* category includes the program team members, the project manager, the performing organization, customers, and potential customers.
- The *monitor with minimum effort* category includes competitors and affected individuals or organizations.

Unlike risks, stakeholders cannot be managed, only stakeholder expectations can be managed.[3] Stakeholders have a different level of engagement. Stakeholders' levels of engagement can be defined as follows:

- *Unaware* is when a stakeholder is not aware of a program and is not engaged with it;
- *Resistant* is when a stakeholder is resistant to a change a program will bring;
- *Neutral* is when a stakeholder is aware of a program, but is not engaged with it or have any influence over a program;
- *Supportive* is when a stakeholder is supportive of a change a program will bring and has influence over a program; and
- *Leading* is when a stakeholder is actively engaged with a program and has the necessary level of influence over it.

A program manager prepares a stakeholder engagement plan and engages stakeholders, changing their level of engagement as needed through the program life cycle. A program manager also works with the stakeholders to manage their conflicting priorities to reach the required level of engagement and secure the necessary level of influence over a program.

Stakeholder Engagement and Conflicting Priorities Management

The primary goal of stakeholder engagement activities is to establish stakeholder alignment to the strategic goals, intended business benefits,

---

[3] PMI. (2013). *The standard for program management* – Third edition. Newtown Square, PA: Author.

program objectives, and success criteria of a program. It involves putting action to the stakeholder strategy through the building of professional relationships to influence for program advocacy and to monitor stakeholder actions, words, and decisions.[4]

Stakeholder Engagement Planning

The *stakeholder engagement planning activity* outlines how all program stakeholders will be engaged throughout the duration of the program. The stakeholder register is analyzed with consideration of the organization's strategic plan, program charter, and program business case to understand the environment in which a program will operate. As a part of the stakeholder analysis and engagement planning, the following aspects for each stakeholder will be considered:

- Organizational culture and acceptance of change;
- Attitudes about the program and its sponsors;
- Expectation of program benefits delivery;
- Degree of support or opposition to the program benefits; and
- Ability to influence the outcome of the program.[5]

Stakeholder Engagement

Similar to many other pieces of a program's information, a list of stakeholders and their roles changes during the program life cycle, as does the stakeholder level of interest and influence. That is why stakeholder engagement is a continuous activity throughout the program life cycle. Stakeholder engagement starts during the definition phase, continues during the benefits delivery phase, and ends during the program closure phase.

During the definition phase, a program manager conducts a stakeholder engagement planning activity. A program manager identifies program stakeholders, creates a stakeholder register, and engages stakeholders.

---

[4] Martinelli, R. J., Waddell, J. M., & Rahschulte, T. J. (2014). *Program management for improved business results.* (2nd ed.). Hoboken, NJ: John Wiley & Sons, Inc.
[5] PMI. (2013). *The standard for program management* – Third edition. Newtown Square, PA: Author.

During the benefits delivery phase, using a stakeholder map, a program manager manages stakeholders. *Stakeholder engagement management* is a process of communicating and working with stakeholders to meet their needs/expectations, address issues as they occur, and foster appropriate stakeholder engagement in project activities throughout the project life cycle.[6]

As part of the stakeholder engagement management process, a program manager compares stakeholders' current engagement levels with the desired engagement levels. A program manager also identifies and implements strategies to increase stakeholder-engagement levels as needed. A program manager engages stakeholders in influencing decisions related to their areas and keeps them updated about a program's progress. Outputs of stakeholder engagement include risk mitigation; updates to the program management plan and program documents; and change requests to the program scope, budget, and time line.

During the program closure phase, a program manager communicates program benefits delivery to the shareholders. The program manager also communicates final program results, including status and on time and on budget benefits delivery.

Stakeholder Conflicting Priorities Management

Stakeholders are almost always engaged in multiple programs within an organization. Thus, they deal with the conflicting priorities and time constraints. Management of conflicting priorities ensures the stakeholders' needed levels of engagement. A program manager manages conflicting stakeholder priorities during all phases of the program utilizing the stakeholder engagement management process.

During the program definition phase, a program manager engages stakeholders and ensures the necessary levels of engagement in a program. During an initial stakeholder engagement, a program manager shares program details with the stakeholders, including defining program benefits. A program manager defines a necessary level of influence over a program with each stakeholder.

---

[6] PMI. (2013). *A guide to the project management body of knowledge (PMBOK® Guide)* – Fifth edition. Newtown Square, PA: Author.

During the benefits delivery phase, a program manager updates stakeholders about a program's progress and benefits delivery. And, a program manager engages stakeholders to mitigate risks and remove barriers.

During the program closure phase, a program manager shares program benefits delivery results with stakeholders and updates stakeholders about the program, including status and on-time and budget benefits delivery.

CHAPTER 6

Program Governance and Team Management

Using the program management continuum, this chapter defines the program governance domain. It illustrates how the organizational structure defines the program governance structure and program governance roles, and shows how each role fits within the program governance structure. The chapter examines how these roles work together as a program team. The chapter also defines three main functional areas within a program team, showing what roles are included in each functional area and what responsibilities each functional area performs. The chapter concludes by describing how a program manager builds, leads, and off-boards a program team.

The chapter includes the following sections:

- Governance structure;
- Governance roles and functions;
- Team responsibilities; and
- Build, lead, and off-board a program team.

Governance Structure

Program governance creates both the structure and practices to guide the program and provide executive leadership, oversight, and control. Strategically, it encompasses the relationship between the oversight effort and the enterprise business direction. Program governance defines all roles and responsibilities, and it encompasses all the decision-making roles and responsibilities involved in program execution.

Programs require a more complex governing structure than projects do, as programs execute fundamental business changes and deliver significant

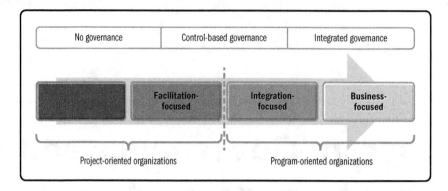

Figure 6-1:   Organizational structure defines program governance structure.[1]

benefits. A simple management structure typically governs projects. A program manager, acting in a role similar to that of the program governance board, provides project oversight and aids with escalation and resolution of risks. The business sponsor may also play a role in governing a project by ensuring that the deliverables align with business strategy.

The program governance structure is defined by an organizational structure and a program management structure. The organizational structure influences the program governance structure in the following key ways:

- Institutes the level of authority and reporting structure within the program;
- Ensures a balance between organizational horizontal and program vertical structures;
- Establishes management structure across business units;
- Aligns program governance board with the organization-wide structure; and
- Defines a program management structure.

A program management structure has an immediate effect on the program governance structure, as the program governance structure is being adopted to the program management structure. To illustrate this point, we will use the program management continuum and show how the program governance structure changes as an organization moves from project-oriented to program-oriented, as shown in Figure 6-1.

---

[1]Martinelli, R. J., Waddell, J. M., & Rahschulte, T. J. (2014). *Program management for improved business results.* (2nd ed.). Hoboken, NJ: John Wiley & Sons, Inc.

If the organization is far left, or administration-focused, it is likely that no formalized program governance model exists, or is needed. For organizations that operate in the middle of the continuum, it is common to see a traditional controlling approach to program-level governance. This is because a single-project approach with traditional project management methods remains the primary philosophy and influence. The collection, analysis, and reporting of project performance data, with the intent to measure conformance, is the primary approach. For program-focused organizations, those operating on the right side of the continuum, an integrated approach to program-level governance is necessary. The integrated approach recognizes the collaborative relationship between the project teams, the program teams, and the business team of an enterprise.[2]

Governance Roles and Functions

Creating a program governance structure involves defining roles, assigning each role a certain program function, and granting each role decision-making authority. Depending on the complexity of a program, the program governance structure includes all or many of the following roles.

The *program sponsor* is the individual responsible for championing the application of organizational resources to the program and for ensuring program success. The program sponsor is frequently a senior executive within the organization who has investment decision-making authority. The program sponsor is personally vested in ensuring the success of the program and may act as a chairperson of the program governance board.

Program governance board members are responsible for authorizing and overseeing a program. As the program evolves, this governing body ensures that it continues to align with the enterprise strategic direction. The board is also responsible for defining and implementing appropriate governance systems and methods. Program governance board members are usually executives who have strategic insight, technical knowledge, functional responsibilities, operational accountabilities, responsibilities for managing the organization's portfolio, and

---

[2] Martinelli, R. J., Waddell, J. M., Rahschulte, T. J. (2014). *Program management for improved business results.* (2nd ed.). Hoboken, NJ: John Wiley & Sons, Inc.

abilities to present to important stakeholder groups. In some organizations, a program governance board is also referred to as a steering committee.

The *program manager* is responsible for management and oversight of the program interactions with the program governance function. The program manager ensures that the program goals remain aligned to the overall strategic objectives of the organization. The program manager is responsible for setting up and managing the program, and for ensuring that it is performing according to plan.

Program team members are responsible for various aspects of the program. They may contribute to the definition of the program strategy or plan, or oversee and coordinate the activities conducted as part of the program plan, including components and program operational management activities. Program team members include subprogram managers and project managers responsible for subprograms and projects that are components of the program. More complex programs may also include program planner, project planner, risk manager, and program management office manager.

The *project manager* is responsible for oversight of a project that is a component of the program. The project manager is ultimately responsible for delivery of the project outputs as defined in the project charter and the program plan. Project manager activities include effective project planning, execution, and tracking.[3]

The *program planner* is responsible for updating program plans and schedules (e.g., Gantt charts to plan and report project progress). This role may exist in more complex programs.

The *project planner* is responsible for updating the project plan and schedules (e.g., Gantt charts to plan and report project progress). This role may exist in more complex projects.

The *risk manager* is responsible for identifying potential risks in advance, analyzing them, and taking precautionary steps to reduce and mitigate the risk.

The *project management office manager* is responsible for defining and maintaining standards for project management within the program. The program management office manager strives to standardize and

---

[3] PMI. (2013). *The standard for program management* – Third edition. Newtown Square, PA: Author.

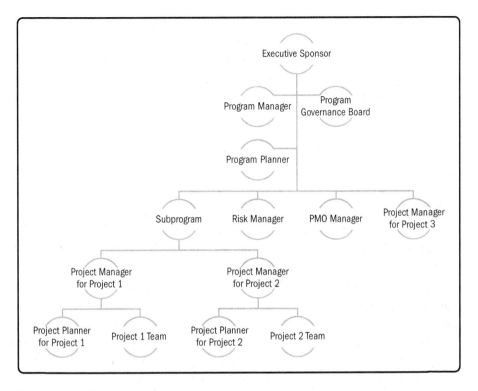

Figure 6-2:   Program governance structure.

introduce economies of repetition in the execution of projects within a program.

Using the call center's process improvement program example, we will create a program governance, as shown in Figure 6-2. The program governance structure uses definitions of the executive sponsor, program governance board, risk manager, and program management office manager roles.

An integrated approach to program-level governance incorporates many elements, with the primary elements centered on three factors:

- Setting and maintaining strategy alignment;
- Reviewing progress; and
- Making decisions that affect program strategy.[4]

---

[4] Martinelli, R. J., Waddell, J. M., & Rahschulte, T. J. (2014). *Program management for improved business results.* (2nd ed.). Hoboken, NJ: John Wiley & Sons, Inc.

Effective governance is critical to program success. Poorly articulated management structure, vaguely defined roles, wrong people appointed to the roles, and overlapping decision-making authority can prevent a program governance body from reaching consensus on critical decisions, and can prevent a program from achieving sustained momentum.

Team Responsibilities

In the previous section, we defined various roles within the program governance structure, including the program sponsor, program governance board members, program manager, program team members, project manager, program planner, project planner, risk manager, and project management office manager. In this section, we will examine how these roles work together as a program team and what responsibilities they perform.

A program team can be broken into three main functional areas, strategy alignment, program management, and program execution. A program sponsor and program governance board members ensure that a program is aligned with the organizational strategy. A program manager and a program management office manage a program. Program team members, project managers, program planner, project planner, and risk manager execute a program. Not all programs have all roles listed, and some programs may have additional roles, as roles and responsibilities may vary in different organizations.

Each of the three functional areas performs a defined set of responsibilities to fulfill its function within a program. To ensure program strategy alignment with the organizational strategy, a program sponsor and program governance board members perform the following responsibilities:

- Provide strategic direction;
- Ensure committed resources;
- Influence teams to remove obstacles;
- Monitor execution and program status; and
- Ensure effective change management.

To manage a program, a program manager and program management office manager perform the following responsibilities:

- Provide program oversight;
- Set up governance structure;

- Deliver status reports;
- Guide project managers;
- Resolve issues and risks; and
- Oversee budget execution.

And, to execute a program, program team members, project managers, program planners, project planners, and risk managers perform the following responsibilities:

- Execute component plans;
- Provide component statuses;
- Manage component risks; and
- Manage component budgets.

Figure 6-3 depicts three main functional areas of the program team, which include strategy alignment, program management, and program execution.

Build, Lead, and Off-Board a Program Team

One of the key responsibilities of a program manager is to build, lead, and off-board a program team. Before examining a program manager role in building, leading, and off-boarding a program team, it is important to

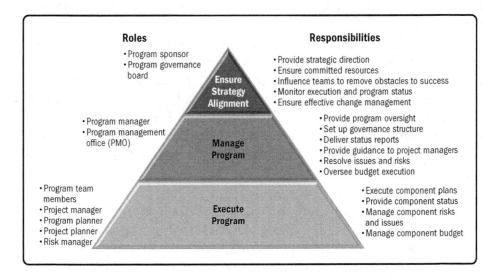

Figure 6-3:   The program team includes three main functional areas.

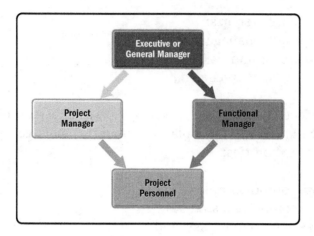

Figure 6-4: Balanced matrix organization.

discuss a matrix organizational structure, in which programs frequently operate. A matrix organization is defined as one in which there is dual or multiple managerial accountability and responsibility, as was previously defined in Chapter 2.

A more detailed definition describes *matrix organizations* as organizations where team members do not report directly to the program manager and are not solely focused on program work. A dual reporting structure and multiple conflicting priorities of team members are two big challenges that a program manager faces today in building and leading a program team.

The matrix organizational form may vary from one in which the project manager holds a very strong managerial position to one in which the project manager plays only a coordinating role. To illustrate the organizational principles, a matrix will be considered first in which there is a balance of power between the project and functional managers. It must be recognized that such a balanced situation, considered by some authorities to be ideal, probably seldom occurs in practice. In a balanced matrix organization, various people in the organization have two bosses, as shown in Figure 6-4.

Implicit in the definition of the matrix organization is the recognition that the project is temporary, whereas the functional departments are more permanent. Although all organizations are temporary in that they are constantly changing, the matrix is designed to be temporary,

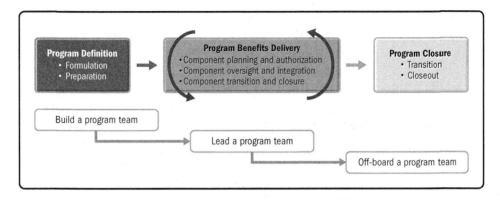

Figure 6-5:   During a program life cycle, a program manager builds, leads, and off-boards a program team.

and a particular organizational structure lasts only for the finite life of the project.[5]

Matrix organizations may impose various conflicts of interest between the program and departmental objectives for team members. For example, a team member may aspire to advance business skills and not project management skills; however, program work requires gaining project management skills. Another example of a conflict may be that a project manager is receiving different directions on how to build a project management plan, as a department and a program may have different requirements as related to the project management plan structure and content.

During the program life cycle, a program manager builds, leads, and off-boards a program team. A program manager starts building a program team early in the program life cycle, during the definition phase. During the program benefits delivery phase, a program manager leads a program team. And, during the closure phase, a program manager off-boards a program team. Figure 6-5 shows activities related to the program team building, leading, and off-boarding.

---

[5] Stuckenbruck, L. C. (1979, September). The matrix organization. *Project Management Quarterly.* Retrieved from https://www.pmi.org/learning/library /matrix-organization-structure-reason-evolution-1837

The program manager can use multiple tools to build a program team as well as to hold team members accountable for timely task execution. Among key team building techniques are:

- Facilitate relationship building;
- Recognize accomplishments and milestones completion; and
- Create ways to celebrate success.

One of the key tools a program manager can use to hold team members accountable for timely task execution is to work with the functional managers to add program goals to team members' performance goals. Other techniques to hold program team members accountable for timely task execution include:

- Conduct regular meetings with each team member to discuss work progress;
- Set deadlines, establish deliverables time lines, and develop guidelines around deliverables execution;
- Establish clear measurement metrics and allowable thresholds;
- Assist team members in learning and advancing their professional knowledge; and
- Assist team members in fulfilling their professional goals within the scope of the program.

The human aspect of team building is really important. That is why a successful program manager needs to establish a personal connection with the team members. If a program team is colocated, a program manager should conduct in-person meetings where possible and may establish a practice of making rounds in the office to talk to program team members.

Many project team members do not work in the same location—even those working in the government sector. Even if they are in the same location, team members rely extensively on virtual communication tools rather than face-to-face communication. Using communication and collaboration technology tools is the norm—and we're not even addressing all the cool software tools designed specifically to manage projects.[6]

---

[6] LaBrosse, M. (n. d.). *Email or phone conference? Making the most of communication technologies in each project phase.* Retrieved from https://www.pmiwdc.org /article/email-or-phone-conference-making-most-communication-technologies

Virtual program management adds additional requirements to building and managing a program team. And, program team building and management take up more of the program manager's time. A program manager may face the virtual team challenges of not having a physical and social presence as well as additional cultural and language barriers. Success in virtual team building and management heavily relies on technology, requires additional program manager proficiencies, and employs supplementary program team building and management techniques.

Effective use of the appropriate technologies during different project phases is crucial to the success of "global project teams," or really, any team in which team members collaborate virtually. In my experience leading a project team collaborating between two continents, I have found that the use of multiple communication technologies— carefully chosen depending on the current project phase—is needed to keep global project teams collaborating effectively and on schedule. Deciding which communication technologies project teams use to collaborate during each of the project phases, and learning to use them most effectively, is key to project success.[7]

A program manager operating in the virtual program environment, may employ supplementary techniques to build trust and motivate a program team:

- Conduct telepresence meetings and video conferences;
- Communicate effectively and regularly, daily via email and a few times a week by phone;
- Conduct in-person team sessions especially early on, during the definition phase; and
- Visit team members in their geographical locations.

---

[7]LaBrosse, M. (n. d.). *Email or phone conference? Making the most of communication technologies in each project phase.* Retrieved from https://www.pmiwdc.org/article/email-or-phone-conference-making-most-communication-technologies

CHAPTER 7

Program Life Cycle Management

This chapter defines the program life cycle domain and outlines a detailed approach to program execution through the program life cycle. A program delivers benefits by executing a set of phases that constitute a program life cycle. A program life cycle includes three phases, definition, benefits delivery, and closure. A purpose of the definition phase is to expand the business case and strategic plan objectives, and fully define expected program outcomes. A purpose of the benefits delivery phase is to integrate and manage program components to facilitate the delivery of the intended program benefits. A purpose of the closure phase is to execute a controlled closure of the program.

The chapter covers the following key aspects:

- Program life cycle phases;
- Definition phase;
- Benefits delivery phase; and
- Closure phase.

Program Life Cycle Phases

Programs are undertaken to deliver benefits by achieving business value and producing anticipated business results. A program delivers benefits by executing a set of phases. This approach is called a program life cycle as was initially defined in Chapter 1: What Is Program Management? A program life cycle includes three phases, definition, benefits delivery, and closure. Each of the three phases includes subphases.

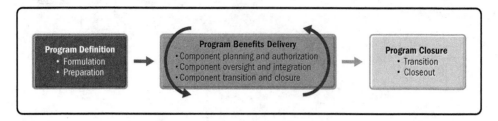

Figure 7-1:   Definition of phases in the program life cycle.

The program definition phase includes two subphases, program formulation and program preparation. During the formulation subphase, a sponsor approves program funding and assigns a program manager. During the preparation subphase, a program manager defines program organization, deploys program teams, and develops the program management plan.

The program benefits delivery phase includes planning, management, and delivery of program components. The program benefits delivery phase is an iterative phase of the program. During this phase, a program manager plans, integrates, and manages program components to facilitate delivery of the intended program benefits.

The program closure phase includes two subphases, the transition and program closeout. During the transition subphase, a program manager coordinates the transitional activities and receives approval to close the program. During the closeout subphase, a program manager performs a set of closeout activities to formally close a program.

A graphical image with details about the phases and subphases of the program life cycle is shown in Figure 7-1.[1]

Definition Phase

The strategic plan determines a need for a program. A program occurs to deliver benefits or to achieve a desired new state. Examples of why programs occur include a launch of a new product, a process improvement, and an implementation of a change. In the call center's process

---

[1] PMI. (2013). *The standard for program management* – Third edition. Newtown Square, PA: Author.

improvement program example, the program occurs to achieve the highest call response quality and fastest call response time.

Before the program's official start, the sponsoring organization may perform some activities, including defining scope, developing concepts and initial requirements, and building acceptable cost guidelines. Deliverables from this predefinition stage of the program may include scope, initial requirements, and cost guidelines documents.

The program definition phase is the first phase of the program life cycle. The purpose of this phase is to expand the business case and strategic plan objectives, and fully define expected program outcomes. The program definition phase includes two subphases, formulation and preparation. During the formulation subphase, the sponsoring organization assigns a program sponsor. A program sponsor performs two key responsibilities, approval of program funding and appointment of a program manager.

During the formulation subphase, a program manager and program sponsor closely work to secure outcomes and produce deliverables that include:

- Secure program funding;
- Define program scope;
- Estimate resources and costs;
- Develop initial risks assessment; and
- Develop a program charter and road map.

Once the program charter is approved, the program moves into the preparation subphase. During this subphase, a program manager defines program organization, deploys the program team, and develops the program management plan. A program manager establishes outcomes and produces deliverables that include:

- Establish a program governance structure;
- Deploy program organization;
- Develop program benefits management strategy; and
- Develop a program management plan.

A *program management plan* is a key document that guides a program manager and a program team through the program life cycle. It uses multiple informational resources, including the program charter, business case, and organizational strategic plan. We will discuss the program management plan in detail in Chapter 8. After the program management plan is approved, the program begins the benefits delivery phase.

Benefits Delivery Phase

The benefits delivery phase is a second and iterative phase of the program life cycle. During this phase, a program manager plans, integrates, and manages program components to facilitate delivery of the intended benefits. A program benefits management strategy is used to guide program execution, as it keeps a program aligned to the desired business results.

One of the common issues that a program manager may encounter during the benefits delivery phase is misalignment between intended business goals and program outputs. To mitigate this issue, a program manager may use a benefits mapping tool that helps ensure that all program components are aligned to the benefits management.

A program manager provides leadership, oversight, and support to successfully execute subprograms and projects within a program. A program manager uses the program management plan as the main tool to ensure delivery of the program benefits.

Program planning has a significant element of uncertainty because a full set of program components may not be known during the definition phase, when the program management plan and road map are initially developed. That is why the benefits delivery phase is an iterative phase. Throughout this phase, a program manager needs to manage program components and, as new information becomes available, replan program components. To accomplish that, the program manager iteratively manages the program components through these three subphases:

- Component planning and authorization;
- Component oversight and integration; and
- Component transition and closure.

Component Planning and Authorization

During the definition phase, the scope of work contains uncertainty and only includes limited information about a program. That is why, during the benefits delivery phase, a program manager formalizes scope of work and integrates new information into component planning. A program manager performs component planning during the benefits delivery phase, as new information about components becomes available and new events require replanning.

In this subphase, a program manager conducts detailed component planning that includes full integration of the components into a program. By doing that, a program manager formalizes scope of work and identifies the deliverables, the completion of which will allow achieving program goals and obtaining program benefits.

Component planning takes place in their plans. The appropriate information from each component's plan is integrated into the program management plan. Upon component planning completion, a program manager verifies that the components properly support program outcomes and approves them for execution.

Component Oversight and Integration

Program components do not produce benefits at the same time. Some components may produce benefits immediately, while other components may need to be integrated before they will produce benefits. Each component's project manager executes an associated component management plan and provides status, risks, and other related information to the program manager, so that component efforts can be integrated into program activities.

It is important to note that program benefits cannot be realized without an integration effort. Individual components can produce their deliverables. However, it is an integration effort that allows delivering the components' deliverables in the coordinated way to realize program benefits. For example, in the call center's process improvement program, each of the two projects—project one, improve call response quality, and project two, decrease call response time—has its deliverables. However, it is an integrated effort of implementing both projects in all call centers that allows for realizing program benefits.

Component Transition and Closure

After a program delivers its intended benefits, it may be transitioned to another organization or closed. Transition to ongoing operations ensures that a program will realize ongoing benefits. Examples of the transition include customer support for a new product or service, change management support, and new product support. In the call center's process improvement program, after projects one and two are implemented in all call centers, there is a need for a transition to the call center's ongoing operations. The transition requires change management support.

Before the end of the benefits delivery phase, all component areas are reviewed to confirm that the benefits were delivered and to transition any remaining activities. The final status is reviewed with the program sponsor and a program governance board before proceeding to the program closure phase.

Closure Phase

The program closure phase is the third and last phase of the program life cycle. The purpose of this phase is to execute a controlled closure of the program. The program is closed by either cancellation or by an approval to close the program after benefits are delivered. A program may be canceled due to a change in the strategic plan or due to poor performance. A program is also closed after a successful completion of all components and delivery of all benefits.

The program closure phase includes two subphases, transition and closeout. During the transition subphase, a program manager coordinates the transitional activities and receives approval to close a program. Before program transition, a program manager, along with the governance board, determine if a program delivered all benefits and all transitional work has been performed. In the latter case, there is work to transition knowledge, resources, and responsibilities. A program manager collects lessons learned, and stores all project-related documentation and artifacts. Historical program information should be used in planning and execution of future programs.

A program manager receives approval to close out a program. During the closeout subphase, a program manager performs a set of closeout activities to close a program formally.

CHAPTER 8

Program Management Infrastructure

This chapter starts by describing how a program manager uses procurement in the delivery of program benefits. The chapter examines program infrastructure, including systems and tools needed to manage a program effectively and describes how to build and maintain a program management plan—a key document that ensures program alignment with the organizational strategy and on-time and on-budget benefits delivery. The chapter analyzes tools for program monitoring and periodic evaluation. It also defines risks and examines risk management and escalation mechanisms. The chapter concludes by describing the program change process, quality control process, and program communication. This chapter can be used as a desktop manual, as it includes multiple program management tools and templates.

The chapter includes the following sections:

- Program procurement planning and execution;
- Infrastructure overview;
- System requirements for effective program execution;
- Program management planning;
- Program monitoring and periodic evaluation;
- Program risk management;
- Change control processes;
- Quality control processes; and
- Program communication.

Program Procurement Planning and Execution

One of the many tools a program manager uses to deliver program benefits is the procurement of products and services. *Program procurement management* addresses the activities necessary to acquire products and services. Program procurement management addresses specific procurement needs that are unique to managing the overall program and the needs of the constituent components. We will use the call center's process improvement program example. During the benefits delivery phase, it was discovered that project two, decrease call response time, required an additional scope. Additional scope includes research around call response time for different call types. It was determined that the research department would perform this task. In this case, the program will procure this research from the research department.

Program procurement includes a few activities that take place during all phases of the program life cycle. Some activities take place on a program level and some on component levels. The procurement process includes:

- Program procurement planning occurs on a program level and takes place during the program definition phase;
- Program procurement administration occurs on the component level with oversight on the program level, and takes place during the program benefits delivery phase; and
- Program procurement closure occurs on the component level with oversight on the program level, and takes place during the program closure phase.

Program Procurement Planning, Administration, and Closure

Program Procurement Planning

Program procurement planning is performed on the program level during the definition phase of the program. A program manager assesses resource requirements for each component and the program as a whole. A program manager assesses commonalities and differences for various procurement activities across the program scope and determines:

- Whether some of the common needs of several individual components could be met with one overall procurement rather than several separate procurement actions;

- The best mix of the types of procurement contracts planned across the program; at the project level, a particular type of contract may be more optimal for that same procurement when viewed at the program level;
- The best program-wide approach to competition; the risks of sole source contracts in one area of the program could be balanced with the different risks associated with full and open competition in other areas of the program; and
- The best program-wide approach to balancing specific external regulatory mandates; for example, rather than setting aside a certain percentage of each contract in the program to meet a small business mandate, it may be more optimal to award one complete contract to achieve the same mandate.[1]

At this stage, a program manager may analyze alternatives. After all information is gathered, a program manager drafts a program procurement plan.

Program Procurement

Procurement should be a centralized function within a program, and it should be conducted on a program level. A program manager sets up procurement standards for the components. The standards include proposal evaluation criteria, qualified seller and buyer lists, and purchase agreements. A program manager establishes proposal evaluation criteria that will be used to evaluate proposals and places requests for quotes (RFQ), requests for proposals (RFP), and invitations for bid (IFB).

Program Procurement Administration

Procurement administration starts after contracts are awarded and performed on the component level. Contract administration and closure are conducted on the component level. Components ensure that contract deliverables are produced on time, deadlines are met, and established quality standards are met. Component project managers report status to a program manager.

---

[1] PMI. (2013). *The standard for program management* – Third edition. Newtown Square, PA: Author.

A program manager maintains oversight of the procurement administration on the program level to ensure that program benefits are realized on time and on budget, and that the quality standards are met across the program.

Program Procurement Closure

Contract closure occurs during the program procurement closure phase and takes place on the component level. After all contract deliverables are produced, component project managers close contracts. At the time of the contract closure, component project managers ensure that all deliverables were produced, that there are no outstanding contract issues, and that all payments were made.

A program manager maintains oversight of the procurement closure on the program level to ensure that program benefits are realized on time and on budget, and that the quality standards are met across the program.

Infrastructure Overview

Program infrastructure provides systems and tools to manage the program effectively. A *system* allows for managing a program management plan and tracking program progress, assigning resources to tasks and analyzing workloads, and managing a budget. *Program tools* include a status report, a risk tracking mechanism, and financial tools. A program manager can perform program operational tasks quicker by utilizing systems and tools. Thus, program infrastructure enables a program manager to lead a program, deliver to the strategic objectives, and become a trusted advisor and subject matter expert.

Program infrastructure may vary significantly among organizations, depending on where organizations operate along the program management continuum. Different use of program management in project-oriented and program-oriented organizations determines the need for the program infrastructure. As the program management function is limited in administration-focused and facilitation-focused organizations, the program execution requires a limited program infrastructure. The need for a more complex program infrastructure increases as organizations move to the right along the program management continuum. As the program management function expands in integration-focused and business-focused organizations, program execution requires a more complex program infrastructure.

Program infrastructure has similarities and differences with the project infrastructure. Similar to projects, programs track budget and actuals, resources, changes, status, and risks. Differently from projects, programs require aggregation of components on a program level. Organizations frequently have a project-centric infrastructure. However, a program manager needs to have a program-centric infrastructure to optimize program operational management and allow sufficient time to a lead a program. The absence of a program-centric infrastructure creates an issue in multiple areas, including budget and actuals, variance analysis, resource management, status report production, issue and risk tracking, and escalation. We will examine the effects in each area in the subsequent sections of this chapter.

Program infrastructure supports program execution throughout the entire program life cycle. During the definition phase, utilizing a system and tools, a program manager develops a program management plan, assigns resources, and develops an initial budget. During the benefits delivery phase, utilizing a system, a program manager maintains a program management plan and tracks program progress. In the program management plan, a program manager also monitors resources' workloads. Using various program tools, a program manager tracks and analyzes program spending, produces status reports, and tracks risks. During the program closeout phase, using program infrastructure, a program manager finalizes the program management plan, off-boards resources, completes the final status report, and closes risks.

System Requirements for Effective Program Execution

System infrastructure is a key element that allows for sustaining the program management discipline. It enables a program manager to lead a program by way of significantly increasing efficiency and ensuring the quality of program execution through automation and consistency around program management plan execution.

Program system support should include an aggregated project plan that allows aggregating project information into a program. It can either be Microsoft Project, spreadsheets, or databases. The system should have the ability to aggregate from multiple projects into program tasks and milestones.[2]

Aggregation of multiple components into a program includes more than just adding or linking components. It includes managing interdependencies between components, managing program-wide milestones, managing program costs, escalating component risks and managing them on a program level, coordinating and prioritizing resources across components, and tracking program operational management tasks.

Project management software can help plan, organize, and manage resource pools and develop resource estimates. Depending on the sophistication of the software, it can manage estimation and planning, scheduling, cost control and budget management, resource allocation, collaboration software, communication, decision making, quality management, and documentation or administration systems. Today, numerous PC- and browser-based project management software and contract management software solutions exist, and are finding applications in almost every organization.

Project management software typically has the following key features:

- Schedule that includes sequence project activities;
- Activity duration, start and finish dates;
- Activity percent completion;
- Resource assignment to the project activities; and
- Project critical path.[3]

Using project management software, a project manager can obtain the following information about a program and components:

- Task completion, in percent;
- Remaining time needed to complete tasks, in days;
- Tasks on, ahead, or behind schedule;
- Resource workloads;
- Overutilized and underutilized resources;

---

[2] Blomquist, T., & Müller, R. (2004). *Program and portfolio managers: Analysis of roles and responsibilities*. Proceedings of the PMI Research Conference (11–14 July), London, England.

[3] Microsoft Project. (n. d.). In *Wikipedia*. Retrieved from https://en.wikipedia.org/wiki/Microsoft_Project

- Program and component risks; and
- Task costs.

Project management software almost always includes various reports that allow tracking task execution, resource workloads, and costs, and identifying risks.

Project management software can be desktop- or web-based. Desktop software is a single-user application that runs on the desktop of an individual user. Desktop software only houses the project management plan and does not have the functionality to support status reports and risk tracking. Desktop software also has a limitation around information sharing, as information can only be shared by exchanging a file with other users.

Web-based software is a multiuser application that can be accessed through a web browser. Web-based software houses not only a project management plan, but also a status report, and has a risk tracker. Web-based software removes the information sharing limitation that desktop software has.

There are many project management systems currently available, including commercial and homegrown products. *Microsoft Project* is one of the most widely used desktop project management systems. Microsoft Project is a project management software program, developed and sold by Microsoft, that is designed to assist a project manager in developing a plan, assigning resources to tasks, tracking progress, managing the budget, and analyzing workloads.[4]

Microsoft Office Project Server is one of the most widely used web-based project management systems. Microsoft Office Project Server is a project management server solution made by Microsoft. It uses Microsoft SharePoint as its foundation, and supports interface from either Microsoft Project as a client application, or by web browser connecting to its Project Web App (PWA) component.[5]

As was mentioned earlier, many organizations have project-centric and not program-centric systems. One of the main limitations that the project-centric system has for program management is an absence of a

---

[4] Microsoft Project. (n. d.). In *Wikipedia*. Retrieved from https://en.wikipedia.org/wiki/Microsoft_Project

[5] Microsoft Project Server. (n. d.). In *Wikipedia*. Retrieved from https://en.wikipedia.org/wiki/Microsoft_Project_Server

mechanism to aggregate component tasks and milestones into a program, and to escalate risks from components to a program level.

System requirements to effectively manage a program should include the following functionality:

- Manage links and interdependencies between components;
- Aggregate component management plans to a program management plan;
- Coordinate and prioritize resources across components;
- Manage program costs;
- Consolidate component status reports to a program status report;
- Escalate component risks to a program level;
- Track program operational management tasks; and
- Develop program reports that allow for tracking task execution, resource workloads, costs, and risks.

The industry-leading project management software program and project management server solutions, Microsoft Project and Microsoft Office Project Server, are both project-centric. The majority of the functionality that these software and server solutions have is geared for managing a project and not a program. They do not have the program-specific functionality described above.

In Microsoft Project, a program management plan may be built using one of two approaches:

- Build a megaprogram management plan where components are included as subplans; or
- Build separate plans and link them using the Microsoft Office "link projects" functionality.

The first option can be executed by creating a megaproject in Microsoft Project and adding multiple work streams to it. A megaproject becomes a program and multiple work streams become components.

Microsoft Project allows linking projects to create a master project. To help keep a large project more organized, you can link several project files together to create a master project/subproject arrangement (also known as external dependencies). For example, a construction master project might have subproject files for plumbing, electrical, and carpentry work.[6] Similar to Microsoft Project, Microsoft Office Project Server allows linking multiple projects into a master project. This is done by creating a master project and linking subprojects to it.

Both approaches, creating one large project with multiple work streams and linking multiple projects into a master project, do not allow the full aggregation necessary for a program management plan. A program manager may encounter multiple issues, including a lack of mechanisms to track cross-functional tasks, managing cross-functional resources, and shifting resources from one component to another.

When linking multiple projects into a master project, information may be duplicated and not aggregated. For example, if you link projects that use the same resources, you will create duplicate resource names, including name, pay rate, and resource calendars, which could be confusing.[7]

System Usage During Program Execution

A system is being used during the entire program life cycle. A system can be Microsoft Project, Microsoft Office Project Server, a spreadsheet, or a database.

Program Definition Phase

During the definition phase, a program manager develops a program management plan. The plan contains tasks and milestones for the components and the program as a whole. This is an initial version of the plan, as a program manager does not have complete information about program components during the program definition phase.

A program manager defines the structure and sets up a program status report that tracks components and program status. Based on the tools available, a status report can be housed on the Microsoft Office Project Server that has a built-in feature for the status report. The status

---

[6] Microsoft Office Support. (n.d.). Retrieved from https://support.office.com /en-us/article/Link-projects-to-create-a-master-project-36bcd34d-db5c-403a-9eca-90e878920f2a?ui=en-US&rs=en-US&ad=US&fromAR=1

[7] Microsoft Office Support. (n.d.). Retrieved from https://support.office.com /en-us/article/Link-projects-to-create-a-master-project-36bcd34d-db5c-403a-9eca-90e878920f2a?ui=en-US&rs=en-US&ad=US&fromAR=1

report can be prepared in Microsoft Word or PowerPoint, and shared on a program site or a shared drive (e.g., on the SharePoint site).

A program manager defines and sets up a risk-tracking mechanism. Based on the tools available, risks can be tracked in the Microsoft Office Project Server, in Excel, or on a SharePoint site. Both Microsoft Office Project Server and SharePoint sites have built-in features that allow tracking risks.

A program manager identifies or sets up reports that will be used to analyze milestones and the task schedule, program and completion risks, program budgets, and more. These reports will also be used for updates to the program management governance board and program team.

Program Benefits Delivery Phase

During the benefits delivery phase, a program manager leads program execution, ensuring it is on time and within budget, by executing a program management plan, preparing status reports, monitoring program reports, and tracking risks. A system plays a vital role during this phase, as it houses some or all of the program documents, including a program management plan, program reports, status reports, and risks.

This phase is an iterative phase of the program. During this phase, a program manager updates the program management plan and budget with component information. As the program manager acquires program resources, he or she assigns resources to the tasks. The project creates budgets based on assignment work and resource rates. As resources are assigned to tasks and assignment work is estimated, the program calculates the cost, equal to the work times the rate, which rolls up to the task level and then to any summary tasks, and finally, to the project level. Resource definitions (people, equipment, and materials) can be shared between projects using a shared resource pool. Each resource can have its calendar, which defines what days and shifts a resource is available. Resource rates are used to calculate resource assignment costs, which are rolled up and summarized at the resource level. Each resource can be assigned to multiple tasks in multiple plans and each task can be assigned multiple resources, and the application schedules task work can be based on the resource availability as defined in the resource calendars. All resources can be defined in the label without limit. Therefore, it cannot determine how many finished products can be produced with a given amount of raw materials. This makes Microsoft Project unsuitable for solving problems of available materials' constrained production.

Additional software is necessary to manage a complex facility that produces physical goods.[8]

Program Closure Phase

During the program closure phase, a program manager ensures that the program delivered all benefits and that program work fully transitioned. A system assists with this work, as a program manager uses the program management plan to confirm that all benefits were delivered as planned and a program was transitioned. A program manager marks all tasks and milestones in the program management plan as complete and runs program reports to perform final analysis around program execution on time and on budget. A program manager also produces a final status report and closes all risks.

Program Management Plan

A program management plan is a key program document. The plan is used during the entire program duration; however, it serves different purposes during each phase. A program management plan's main purpose is to ensure program alignment with the organizational strategy. As was mentioned earlier, some organizations do not follow through on the execution of the strategic plan, which then does not fully cascade down to the program level. During the program definition phase, to ensure program alignment with the organizational strategy, a program management plan should use a strategic plan as an input document.

Sometimes, organizations do not establish tracking mechanisms to ensure on-time and on-budget program delivery. During the benefits delivery phase, a program manager should establish mechanisms to ensure the program's timely execution. Mechanisms should include program reports that allow for tracking timely task execution, full resource utilization, and on-budget delivery.

Upon program completion, some organizations do not fully incorporate benefits realized through program execution and do not align the ongoing operations with implemented changes. During the program closure phase, using the program management plan, a program

---

[8] Microsoft Project. (n. d.). In *Wikipedia*. Retrieved from https://en.wikipedia. org/wiki/Microsoft_Project

manager ensures a smooth transition of the delivered program benefits to ongoing operations.

A program management plan can be built using one of the two approaches, activity-based and resource-based. A *resource-based approach* to building a program management plan assigns resources to tasks, estimates hours of work based on task duration, and calculates program costs such as the product of hours multiplied by resource rates. An advantage of this approach is that it allows for building a full set of program tasks and accurately estimates their duration and cost. A disadvantage of this approach is the time required to build a list of tasks and identify and assign resources to them. For example, adding resources to the plan in Microsoft Project may be a time-consuming and laborious task. Another disadvantage of this approach is that, initially, the program management plan may be incomplete, as the full set of the program components may not be known early in the program life cycle.

An *activity-based approach* to building a program management plan uses tasks, duration, and cost from a similar program or a component. This information can be obtained using programs executed in the past or industry best practices. An advantage of this approach is that it allows obtaining tasks, duration, and cost information early. And, using historical knowledge from other programs or industry best practices, this approach allows creating a more comprehensive program management plan early in the program life cycle when a full set of components of the current program may not be known. A disadvantage of this approach is that it may have discrepancies in the tasks, duration, and cost, as other programs or industry best practices may not be the same as a current program.

Program cost can be calculated using one of the two approaches, resources' hourly rates that calculate task costs and historical information that is used to estimate task costs. Calculating program costs using the resources approach includes adding resources in the program management plan using the following steps:

- Click the View tab. In the Resource Views group, click Resource Sheet;
- In the Resource Name field, type work, material, or generic resource name;
- If you want to designate resource groups, then in the Group field for the resource name, type the name of the group;

- Specify the resource type:
  - To specify that this resource is a work resource, in the Type field, click Work;
  - To specify that this resource is a material resource, in the Type field, click Material. In the Material Label field, type the label (e.g., yards, tons, or boxes) for the resource;
  - To specify that this resource is a cost resource, in the Type field, click Cost;
- In the Max Units field for the resource, type the number of total units of this resource that is available for this project. The maximum units' value specifies how much of this resource is available for this project (e.g., part time or multiples). For example, if you have a resource who is available for your project two days a week, you can enter a maximum units' value of 40%. You can use maximum units to specify multiple availabilities of a resource designation. For example, suppose you have a resource named Engineers, a single resource that represents three individual engineers on your team. You can enter the maximum units for Engineers as 300%. You can schedule all three engineers for full-time work at one time without the Engineers resource being over-allocated. You can enter maximum units as a percentage (e.g., 50%, 100%, 300%), or as a decimal (e.g., 0.5, 1, 3).
- To create a budget resource, select the resource, right-click the resource name, and then click Information. Select the Budget check box.

You can add a work resource and associated information by using the managing application programming interface (MAPI) email address book, from the Active Directory, or from Microsoft Project Server. Click the Resource tab, and in the Insert group, click Add Resources. Click Build Team from Enterprise (Project Professional only), Active Directory, or Address Book.[9]

---

[9] Support Microsoft Office. (n.d.). Retrieved from https://support.office.com/en-us/article/Add-resources-to-your-project-1a744960-d960-426a-b687-e42ba3f6c0cb

A program management plan structure should include all parameters necessary to track successful program benefits execution and effectively communicate program status to the program governance board and program team. The program management plan may include the following columns: program time line, task order number, work breakdown structure (WBS), task name, task percent complete, task duration in days, start date, finish date, predecessor activity, resources, actual start date, actual finish date, and Gantt chart.

A *time line* is a way of displaying a list of events in chronological order, sometimes described as a project artifact. It is typically a graphic design showing a long bar labeled with dates alongside itself and usually events labeled on points where they would have happened.[10] In the program management world, a program time line is a useful tool to get a program-wide view of critical task duration and milestone dates. It is also a communication tool to provide status updates to the program governance board and the program team. To add a task or a milestone to the time line, right click on the task and choose Add to time line in the drop-down box.

A *task order number* is a number in the leftmost column that lists task numbers in order starting with one. Typically, a program management plan is large and includes hundreds of rows. A task order number helps quickly find a task and is used to list a predecessor activity for the current task.

The *work breakdown structure* (WBS) column shows a hierarchical decomposition of the total scope of work to be carried out by the project team to accomplish the project objectives and create the required deliverables.[11] It is a tree structure, which shows a subdivision of effort required to achieve an objective (e.g., a program, project, and contract).[12]

A *task name* displays the name of a task. It is a text box that allows typing any text, adjusting fonts, and applying formatting. A task can be an independent task, a summary task, or a subtask. A summary task has subtasks underneath it and shows their combined information.

---

[10] Timeline. (n.d.). In *Wikipedia*. Retrieved from https://en.wikipedia.org/wiki/Timeline

[11] PMI. (2015). *PMI lexicon of project management terms, Version 3.0*. Newtown Square, PA: Author.

[12] Work breakdown structure. (n.d.). In *Wikipedia*. Retrieved from https://en.wikipedia.org/wiki/Work_breakdown_structure

To create a subtask in the Gantt Chart view, select the task you want to turn into a subtask, then click Task > Indent.

The *task percent complete* column shows partial or full completion of a task in a percent value. Based on task percent complete, Microsoft Project and other systems calculate component and program percent complete to date. It is a very useful measure of the components and the overall program's progress.

The *duration* column shows the total number of work periods required to complete an activity or work breakdown structure component, expressed in hours, days, or weeks.[13] Duration is calculated as a sum of the business days between task start and finish dates.

A *start date* column displays the first day when a task execution is scheduled to start. It serves as a baseline for a comparison with a task actual start date. A task may start on, ahead, or later than a scheduled start date. If a task starts ahead or later than scheduled, it leads to a variance between a start and actual start dates.

A *finish date* column displays the last day when a task execution is scheduled to complete. It serves as a baseline to compare with an actual finish date. A task may finish on, ahead, or later than a scheduled finish date. If a task finishes ahead or later than a scheduled finish date, it leads to a variance between a finish and actual finish dates.

A *predecessor activity* column shows an activity that logically comes before a dependent activity on a schedule.[14] Predecessor activity lists a task or tasks that must be completed before the start of a current task. In Microsoft Project, predecessor activities are listed as task order numbers separated by a comma.

A *resources* column lists program or component resources. Resources are typically people included in your project plan, whether or not they are assigned to tasks.[15] Resources can be broken into three categories,

---

[13] PMI. (2015). *PMI lexicon of project management terms, Version 3.0.* Newtown Square, PA: Author.

[14] PMI. (2015). *PMI lexicon of project management terms, Version 3.0.* Newtown Square, PA: Author.

[15] Microsoft Office Support. (n.d.). Retrieved from https://support.office.com /en-us/article/Add-resources-to-your-project-1a744960-d960-426a-b687-e42ba3f6c0cb

enterprise resources, non-enterprise resources, and generic resources. An *enterprise resource* is part of the list of resources for the whole organization; therefore, each of these resources can be shared across multiple projects. Typically, the list of enterprise resources is managed by an administrator, and each project manager adds these resources to their projects as needed. A *non-enterprise resource,* or local resource, is not part of the list of resources for the whole organization. No other project manager can use your non-enterprise resources in their projects. *Generic resources* are used to specify the staffing requirements for a project, such as carpenters and developers, or a team of resources.[16]

An *actual start date* column displays a date when a task starts. As was described above, a task may start on, ahead of, or later than a scheduled date. A variance that compares actual and scheduled task start dates allows for determining if a task started before or later than scheduled. If a task started ahead of schedule, a program manager needs to decide on the early start of a subsequent task. And if a task started later than scheduled, a program manager needs to prepare a mitigation plan to ensure that a subsequent task will start on schedule.

An *actual finish date* column displays a date when a task is completed. As was described above, a task may finish on, ahead of, or later than a scheduled date. A variance that compares actual and scheduled task finish dates allows for determining if a task is finished before or later than scheduled. If a task is finished ahead of schedule, a program manager needs to decide on an early start of a subsequent task. And if a task is finished later than scheduled, a program manager needs to prepare a mitigation plan to ensure that a subsequent task will start on schedule.

A *Gantt chart* is a bar chart of schedule information where activities are listed on the vertical axis, dates are shown on the horizontal axis, and activity durations are shown as horizontal bars placed according to start and finish dates.[17] A Gantt chart shows all program and component tasks durations, milestones, and interdependencies.

---

[16] Microsoft Office Support. (n.d.). Retrieved from https://support.office.com/en-us/article/Add-resources-to-your-project-1a744960-d960-426a-b687-e42ba3f6c0cb

[17] PMI. (2015). *PMI lexicon of project management terms, Version 3.0.* Newtown Square, PA: Author.

A program management plan is developed at the component level and is aggregated at the program level. It includes component and sub-program plans as well as program operational management activities. At the component level, a program management plan facilitates management of program scope, costs, schedule, resources, and risks. At the program level, a program management plan facilitates interaction with components to manage changes and mitigate risks and enables component alignment to deliver program benefits.

Each component has an associated component management plan. A component management plan may include a project management plan, a transition plan, an operational plan, a maintenance plan, or another type of plan depending upon the type of work under consideration. The appropriate information from each component plan is integrated into the associated plan for the program. This includes information used by the program to help manage and oversee the overall program.[18]

The program management plan is utilized differently in each phase of the program life cycle. A program manager builds the plan during the program definition phase, updates it during the program benefits delivery phase, and closes it during the program closure phase. Using the call center's process improvement program, we will illustrate the program management plan evolution during the program life cycle. All definitions stated above will be graphically illustrated in the program management plan figures presented in the next sections.

Program Definition Phase

During program preparation, a subphase of the program definition phase, a program manager develops a program management plan. Input documents to the plan include a strategic plan, a business case, a program charter, a program business case, a program road map, environmental analysis, and other outputs from the formulation subphase of the program definition phase. The plan may include components' management plans that are needed to achieve desired organizational benefits. And, as not all components' information may be known during

---

[18] PMI. (2013). *The standard for program management* – Third edition. Newtown Square, PA: Author.

the program definition phase, the components' management plans may initially include some, but not all, information.

We will use the call center's process improvement program example. The program includes four components—subprogram one that includes projects one and two, project three, and program operational management. The program is scheduled to start on 3 October 2016 and end on 29 September 2017.

- Subprogram one includes projects one and two. The projects are executed consecutively. Subprogram one is scheduled to start on 3 October 2016 with the start of project one. Subprogram one is scheduled to end on 31 March 2017 with the completion of project two:
  - ○ Project one: Improve call response quality has a duration of three months. It is scheduled to start on 3 October 2016 and end on 30 December 2016. It has multiple resources, project manager one and project team one;
  - ○ Project two: Decrease call response time has a duration of three months. It is scheduled to start on 2 January 2017 and end on 31 March 2017. It has multiple resources, project manager two and project team two.
- Project three: Implement projects one and two has a duration of six months. It is scheduled to start on 3 April 2017 and end on 29 September 2017. It has multiple resources, project manager three, project team three, and call center directors; and
- Program operational management has a duration of twelve months, during an entire program life cycle. It is scheduled to start on 3 October 2016 and end on 29 September 2017. It has one resource, a program manager.

If we use an approach of developing a megaprogram management plan where the subprogram and projects are included as subplans, the initial program management plan will have a structure that is shown in Figure 8-1. The section on top of the program management plan represents a program time line. The plan includes the following columns, descriptions of which were given in the previous section: task order number, WBS, task name, percent complete, duration, start date, finish date, predecessor, and resources.

WBS	Task Name	% Work Complete	Duration	Start	Finish	Predec.	Resource Names	Add New Column
1	**Call Center Process Improvement Program**	0%	260 days	Mon 10/3/16	Fri 9/29/17			
1.1	**SubProgram 1:**	0%	130 days	Mon 10/3/16	Fri 3/31/17			
1.1.1	**Project 1: Improve call response quality**	0%	65 days	Mon 10/3/16	Fri 12/30/16			
1.1.1.1	Project 1 Definition Phase	0%	15 days	Mon 10/3/16	Fri 10/21/16		Project Manager 1, Project Team 1	
1.1.1.2	Project 1 Benefits Delivery Phase	0%	30 days	Mon 10/24/16	Fri 12/2/16	4	Project Manager 1, Project Team 1	
1.1.1.3	Project 1 Closure Phase	0%	20 days	Mon 12/5/16	Fri 12/30/16	8	Project Manager 1, Project Team 1	
1.1.2	**Project 2: Decrease call response time**	0%	65 days	Mon 1/2/17	Fri 3/31/17			
1.1.2.1	Project 2 Definition Phase	0%	14 days	Mon 1/2/17	Thu 1/19/17			
1.1.2.2	Project 2 Benefits Delivery Phase	0%	27 days	Mon 1/23/17	Tue 2/28/17	16	Project Manager 2, Project Team 2	
1.1.2.3	Project 2 Closure Phase	0%	23 days	Wed 3/1/17	Fri 3/31/17	20	Project Manager 2, Project Team 2	
1.2	**Project 3: Implement Projects 1 and 2**	0%	130 days	Mon 4/3/17	Fri 9/29/17	15, 3		
1.2.1	Project 3 Definition Phase	0%	20 days	Mon 4/3/17	Fri 4/28/17			
1.2.2	Project 3 Benefits Delivery Phase	0%	89 days	Mon 5/1/17	Thu 8/31/17	28	Project Manager 3, Call Center Directors, Project Team 3	
1.2.3	Project 3 Closure Phase	0%	21 days	Fri 9/1/17	Fri 9/29/17	32	Project Manager 3, Call Center Directors, Project Team 3	
1.3	**Program Operational Management**	0%	260 days?	Mon 10/3/16	Fri 9/29/17			
1.3.1	Program Operational Management Definition	0%	21 days	Mon 10/3/16	Mon 10/31/16		Program Manager	
1.3.2	Program Operational Management Benefits Delivery Phase	0%	199 days	Tue 11/1/16	Fri 8/4/17	40	Program Manager	
1.3.3	Program Operational Management Closure Phase	0%	40 days?	Mon 8/7/17	Fri 9/29/17	44	Program Manager	

Figure 8-1: The program management plan is built as a megaproject during the program definition phase.

A task can be scheduled either manually or automatically. *Manually scheduled tasks* have a user-defined start, finish, and duration values. The project will never change their dates, but may warn you if there are potential issues with the entered values. *Automatically scheduled tasks* have start, finish, and duration values calculated by Microsoft Project based on dependencies, constraints, calendars, and other factors.[19]

The *baseline* is the approved version of a work product that can be changed using formal change control procedures and is used as the basis for comparison to actual results.[20] Baseline plays an important part in measuring program performance. Throughout the program benefits delivery phase, a program manager calculates schedule and cost variances to compare baseline to actual schedule and cost, and determine if the program is on schedule and budget. Various types of program management software allow setting a baseline. In Microsoft Project, to set the baseline, a program manager needs to click Project > Set Baseline > Set Baseline.

The *project critical path* is the sequence of activities that represents the longest path through a project, which determines the shortest possible duration.[21] Critical path allows calculating the shortest and absolute required time to execute a project. In Microsoft Project, to calculate a component and a critical program path in the context of all tasks, a program manager needs to click View > More Views > Detail Gantt > Apply. To view only critical tasks, a program manager needs to click View > Gantt Chart > Critical in the filter list, as the filter list by default shows all tasks.

Just like projects, programs have a critical path, which goes through component critical paths. The program critical path allows identifying critical components, the execution of which is essential for program

---

[19] Microsoft Office Support. (n.d.). Retrieved from https://support.office.com/en-us/article/How-Project-schedules-tasks-Behind-the-scenes-df3431ab-8d8a-4047-afc6-a87b547dbac0

[20] PMI. (2015). *PMI lexicon of project management terms, Version 3.0*. Newtown Square, PA: Author.

[21] PMI. (2015). *PMI lexicon of project management terms, Version 3.0*. Newtown Square, PA: Author.

success. If a program is experiencing a delay due to a component's execution actual time being longer than scheduled or a resource constraint, a program manager needs to shift resources from non-critical to critical components.[22]

The program critical path can serve as an implementation checklist, as it lists all critical tasks without the completion of which a program cannot be executed. An *implementation checklist* defines the steps required to implement the end state in this specific environment successfully.[23] The implementation checklist may also be referred to as a program readiness checklist.

The application creates critical path schedule, and critical chain and event chain methodology; third-party add-ons also are available. Schedules can be resource-leveled, and chains are visualized in a Gantt chart. Additionally, Microsoft Project can recognize different classes of users. These different classes of users can have differing access levels to projects, views, and other data. Custom objects, such as calendars, views, tables, filters, and fields are stored in an enterprise global, which is shared by all users.[24]

The call center program management plan shown in Figure 8-1 is built using a megaprogram management plan approach, wherein the plan components are listed as subprojects in one megaprogram management plan. In Microsoft Project, a program management plan can also be built by creating component management plans in separate Microsoft Project files and linking them to a program management plan.

Once component management plans are built, a program manager needs to store them in the same folder or a shared directory, for example, a SharePoint site. This step is necessary for the Microsoft Project link project plan function to work. A program manager consolidates

---

[22] Written in collaboration with Sankaran Ramani, MoP, MSP, P3O, CM, PMP, PgMP, PfMP, Director, GRT Consulting LLP
[23] Gardner, D. G. (2001). *Operational readiness—Is your system more "ready" than your environment?* Retrieved from https://www.pmi.org/learning/library/operational-readiness-system-ready-environment-7946
[24] Microsoft Project. (n. d.). In *Wikipedia*. Retrieved from https://en.wikipedia.org/wiki/Microsoft_Project

component management plans into a program management plan using the Microsoft Project link plans function, following these steps:

- Create separate project files for each component, then open or create the project file that you want to be the master project;
- In the master project, click View > Gantt Chart;
- In the Task Name field, click the row below which you want to insert the subproject;
- Click Project > Subproject;
- Click the Project ribbon tab to show the Insert subproject command;
- In the Insert Project box, select the subproject you want to insert;
  - To insert multiple subprojects, hold down Ctrl and click the subprojects in the order that you want to insert them;
  - In most cases, you will want to leave the Link to Project box checked, so that changes in the subproject are reflected in the master project, and vice-versa. But if you just want to copy the subproject into the master project without the files being dynamically linked, uncheck the box; and
- To insert a project in read-only format, click the arrow on the Insert button, and then click Insert Read-Only. Inserting a project read-only creates a link between the two projects, but prevents you from updating the subproject from within the master project. If you update the subproject file directly, however, its changes are reflected in the master project. The Insert Read-Only option is only available when the Link to Project box is checked.[25]

To illustrate how to build a program plan using the Microsoft Project link plans function, we will use the call center's process improvement program as an example. The program includes three major components, subprogram one that includes projects one and two, project three, and program operational management. We will build individual component

---

[25] Microsoft Office Support. (n.d.). Retrieved from https://support.office.com /en-us/article/Link-projects-to-create-a-master-project-36bcd34d-db5c-403a-9eca-90e878920f2a

	❶	Task Mode ▾	Task Name ▾	Duration ▾	Start ▾	Finish ▾
1	🗐	▥	▷ SubProgram 1: Project 1 and 2	130 days?	Mon 10/3/16	Fri 3/31/17
2	🗐	▥	▷ Project 3: Implement Projects 1 and 2	130 days	Mon 4/3/17	Fri 9/29/17
3	🗐	▥	▷ Program Operational Management	260 days?	Mon 10/3/16	Fri 9/29/17

Figure 8-2: Program management plans can be built by linking component management plans.

management plans for each component and store files in the same directory, folder, or shared drive. We will then create a program plan file. And, using the link plans function, we will link all component management plans into one program plan, as shown in Figure 8-2.

The plan includes the following columns: task order number, indicator, task mode, task name, duration, start date, and finish date. The *indicators* column shows that the component management plans are linked to the program management plan. The *task mode* column shows if a task is scheduled manually or automatically.

Manually scheduled tasks have user-defined start, finish, and duration values. Manually scheduled tasks are noted by a green pin sign in the task mode column. Duration of the manually scheduled tasks is set as a text value, for example, today or tomorrow. Manually scheduled tasks are not visualized in a Gantt chart. *Automatically scheduled tasks* have start, finish, and duration values calculated by Microsoft Project based on dependencies, constraints, calendars, and other factors. Automatically scheduled tasks are noted by a blue bar sign in the task mode column, as shown in Figure 8-2. Duration of the automatically scheduled tasks is set as a number value, for example, 130 days. Automatically scheduled tasks are visualized in a Gantt chart.

Once component management plans are linked to the program management plan, updates to the component management plans are automatically processed in the linked program management plan. To view component management plans, expand each plan by clicking on an arrow at the start of the task name.

Program Benefits Delivery Phase

As was mentioned previously, program planning has a significant element of uncertainty. A full set of program components is not known during the program definition phase, when a program management plan is initially developed. That is why program management plan development is an iterative activity.

During the program benefits delivery phase, a program manager needs to manage program components and, as new information becomes available, replan program components and their integration. If needed, a program manager may change program direction. To accomplish that, the program manager iteratively manages the program components through these three subphases:

- Component planning and authorization;
- Component oversight and integration; and
- Component transition and closure.

Component Planning and Authorization

Component planning is performed throughout the duration of the program benefits delivery phase in response to events that require significant replanning or a new component's initiation request. Component planning includes the activities needed to integrate the component into a program to position each component for successful execution. These activities involve formalizing the scope of the work to be accomplished by each of the components and identifying the deliverables that will satisfy the program's goals and benefits.[26]

During the component planning and authorization subphase, the following activities may be performed in the program management plan:

- Update the plan with the new tasks in response to the new components' initiation requests;
- Update existing tasks in response to replanning;
- Integrate components into a program management plan, including identifying, unifying, and coordinating activities within a program management plan as well as making trade-offs among competing objectives and managing interdependencies between knowledge areas; and
- Baseline a program management plan and calculate a critical program path.

---

[26] PMI. (2013). *The standard for program management* – Third edition. Newtown Square, PA: Author.

To illustrate how the plan is being updated with the new tasks, we will use the call center's process improvement program example. During quarter one, it was identified that project two, decrease call response time, required an additional scope. Additional scope includes research around call response time for different call types. Project two's plan was updated to include a new task for research around call response time for different call types. It was determined that the research department would perform this task. The new task addition will be shown on line 21 in Figure 8-3, presented in the next section.

Component Oversight and Integration

In the context of a program, some components produce benefits immediately, while other components need to be integrated before the associated benefits can be realized. For example, in the call center's process improvement program, subprogram one that includes project one, improve call response quality, and project two, decrease call response time, produces benefits immediately. While project three, implement projects one and two, to realize associated benefits, needs to be integrated and implemented in all call centers.

During the component oversight and integration subphase, the following activities may be performed in the program management plan:

- Update program management plan with actual start and finish dates to track when tasks actually started and finished;
- Compare actual start and finish dates with scheduled start and finish dates to identify tasks that started and finished later than scheduled;
- Track program and component progress by calculating tasks partial and full percent completion;
- Track milestone completion;
- Rebaseline program management plan. Microsoft Project allows setting as many as eleven baselines;
- Calculate program and component critical paths;
- Identify program-wide conflicts and interdependencies using the program management plan and program time line;
- Provide program and component status updates; and
- Monitor benefits delivery progress.

WBS	To	Task Name	% Work Complete	Duration	Start	Finish	Predec	Resource Names	Actual Start	Actual Finish
1	1	◢ Call Center Process Improvement Program	10%	260 days?	Mon 10/3/16	Fri 9/29/17			Fri 1/1/16	NA
2	1.1	◢ SubProgram 1:	41%	130 days?	Mon 10/3/16	Fri 3/31/17			Fri 4/1/16	NA
3	1.1.1	◢ Project 1: Improve call response quality	100%	65 days?	Mon 10/3/16	Fri 12/30/16			Mon 10/3/16	Fri 12/30/16
4	1.1.1.1	▷ Program Definition	100%	15 days	Mon 10/3/16	Fri 10/21/16		Project Manager 1, Project Team 1	Mon 10/3/16	Fri 10/21/16
8	1.1.1.2	▷ Benefits Delivery Phase	100%	30 days?	Mon 10/24/16	Fri 12/2/16	4	Project Manager 1, Project Team 1	Mon 10/24/16	Fri 12/2/16
13	1.1.1.3	▷ Program Closure Phase	100%	20 days?	Mon 12/5/16	Fri 12/30/16	8	Project Manager 1, Project Team 1	Mon 12/5/16	Fri 12/30/16
15	1.1.2	◢ Project 2: Decrease call response time	12%	65 days?	Mon 1/2/17	Fri 3/31/17			Fri 4/1/16	NA
16	1.1.2.1	▷ Program Definition	100%	14 days	Mon 1/2/17	Thu 1/19/17		Project Manager 2, Project Team 2	Mon 1/2/17	Thu 1/19/17
20	1.1.2.2	◢ Benefits Delivery Phase	0%	27 days?	Mon 1/23/17	Tue 2/28/17	16	Project Manager 2, Project Team 2	NA	NA
21	1.1.2.2.1	Research around call response time for different call types	0%	15 days	Mon 1/23/17	Fri 2/10/17		Research Department		
22	1.1.2.2.2	Review current processes	0%	1 day	Mon 2/13/17	Mon 2/13/17	21	Project Team 2	NA	NA
23	1.1.2.2.3	Identify gaps	0%	5 days	Tue 2/14/17	Mon 2/20/17	22	Project Team 2	NA	NA
24	1.1.2.2.4	Develop future state process flows	0%	5 days	Tue 2/21/17	Mon 2/27/17	23	Project Team 2	NA	NA
25	1.1.2.2.5	Review future state process flows and gain approval	0%	1 day	Tue 2/28/17	Tue 2/28/17	24	Project Team 2	NA	NA
26	1.1.2.2.6	Milestone: Future state process flows are complete	0%	0 days	Tue 2/28/17	Tue 2/28/17	25	Project Team 2	NA	NA
27	1.1.2.3	▷ Program Closure Phase	0%	23 days	Wed 3/1/17	Fri 3/31/17	20	Project Manager 2, Project Team 2	NA	NA
29	1.2	◢ Project 3: Implement Projects 1 and 2	0%	130 days	Mon 4/3/17	Fri 9/29/17	15,3		NA	NA
30	1.2.1	▷ Program Definition	0%	20 days	Mon 4/3/17	Fri 4/28/17		Project Manager 3, Call Center Directors, Project Team 3	NA	NA
34	1.2.2	▷ Benefits Delivery Phase	0%	89 days	Mon 5/1/17	Thu 8/31/17	30	Project Manager 3, Call Center Directors, Project Team 3	NA	NA
39	1.2.3	▷ Program Closure Phase	0%	21 days	Fri 9/1/17	Fri 9/29/17	34	Project Manager 3, Call Center Directors, Project Team 3	NA	NA
41	1.3	◢ Program Operational Management	0%	260 days?	Mon 10/3/16	Mon 10/31/16			NA	NA
42	1.3.1	▷ Program Definition	0%	21 days?	Mon 10/3/16	Mon 10/31/16		Program Manager	NA	NA
46	1.3.2	▷ Benefits Delivery Phase	0%	199 days?	Tue 11/1/16	Fri 8/4/17	42	Program Manager	NA	NA
51	1.3.3	▷ Program Closure Phase	0%	40 days?	Mon 8/7/17	Fri 9/29/17	46	Program Manager	NA	NA

Schedule is within 0.5% of the finish date
Schedule is within 1.5% of the finish date
Schedule is within 2.5% of the finish date
Schedule is within 3.5% of the finish date

Figure 8-3:   The program management plan is regularly updated during the benefits delivery phase.

All component information becomes known during the program benefits delivery phase. During the component planning and authorization subphase of the benefits delivery phase, a program management plan is updated with all components' information. During the component oversight and integration subphase of the benefits delivery phase, a program management plan is used to track tasks' partial and full percent completion, as shown in Figure 8-3.

During the program benefits delivery phase, component planning and authorization, and component oversight and integration subphases, a program management plan may include the following columns:

- Text column shows components' task status indicators using smiley face images:
  - Green smiley face depicts that schedule is within 0.5% of the finish date;
  - Blue smiley face depicts that schedule within 1.5% of the finish date;
  - Yellow smiley face depicts that schedule within 2.5% of the finish date; and
  - Red smiley face depicts that schedule within 3.5% of the finish date;
- Actual start date column shows actual start dates for each task;
- Actual finish date column shows actual finish dates for each task; and
- Task number, task name, percent complete, start and finish, predecessor, resources columns, and Gantt chart, were described in the previous section.

During the component oversight and integration subphase, a program manager tracks component tasks' partial and full completion and utilizes multiple tools within the program management plan:

- Calculate task's partial and full percent complete;
- Track task status depicted by the status indicators, green, blue, yellow, and red smiley faces;
- Calculate variance by comparing actual start date with the scheduled start date and determining if an actual start date is ahead of, on time, or behind a scheduled start date;

- Calculate variance by comparing actual finish date with the scheduled finish date and determining if an actual finish is ahead of, on time, or behind a scheduled finish date;
- Review program time line and identify tasks that are behind schedule; and
- Use reports to track timely benefits delivery, as will be discussed in detail in the next section.

Component Transition and Closure

After program components' successful delivery of their products, services, or results, they may be closed or transitioned into another organization and then closed. Transition addresses the need for ongoing activities, such as product support, service management, change management, user engagement, or customer support from a program component to an operational support function for the ongoing benefits to be achieved.[27] For example, in the call center's process improvement program, after projects one and two are implemented in all call centers, they become a part of their ongoing operations. At that time, the call center's process improvement program and component tasks should be closed.

During the component transition and closure subphase, the following activities may be performed in the program management plan, as shown on Figure 8-4:

- Review all components to verify that the benefits were delivered;
- Transition component activities;
- Mark all program and component tasks as complete in the percent complete column; and
- Create a final program status report using program time line and program reports.

During the program benefits delivery phase, component transition, and closure subphase, a program management plan marks all tasks as 100% complete. A program manager analyzes components' actual start and finish dates, and compares them with the scheduled start and finish

---

[27] PMI. (2013). *The standard for program management* – Third edition. Newtown Square, PA: Author.

	WBS	Task Name	% Work Complet	Duration	Start	Finish	Predec	Resource Names	Actual Start	Actual Finish
1	1	Call Center Process Improvement Program	100%	260 days?	Mon 10/3/16	Fri 9/29/17			Fri 1/1/16	Fri 9/29/17
2	1.1	SubProgram 1:	100%	130 days	Mon 10/3/16	Fri 3/31/17			Mon 1/4/16	Fri 3/31/17
3	1.1.1	Project 1: Improve call response quality	100%	65 days?	Mon 10/3/16	Fri 12/30/16			Mon 1/4/16	Fri 12/30/16
4	1.1.1.1	Project 1 Definition Phase	100%	15 days?	Mon 10/3/16	Fri 10/21/16		Project Manager 1, Project Team 1	Mon 1/4/16	Fri 10/21/16
8	1.1.1.2	Project 1 Benefits Delivery Phase	100%	30 days?	Mon 10/24/16	Fri 12/2/16	4	Project Manager 1, Project Team 1	Mon 1/25/16	Fri 12/2/16
13	1.1.1.3	Project 1 Closure Phase	100%	20 days?	Mon 12/5/16	Fri 12/30/16	8	Project Manager 1, Project Team 1	Mon 3/7/16	Fri 12/30/16
15	1.1.2	Project 2: Decrease call response time	100%	65 days	Mon 1/2/17	Fri 3/31/17			Fri 4/1/16	Fri 3/31/17
16	1.1.2.1	Project 2 Definition Phase	100%	14 days?	Mon 1/2/17	Thu 1/19/17		Project Manager 2, Project Team 2	Fri 4/1/16	Thu 1/19/17
20	1.1.2.2	Project 2 Benefits Delivery Phase	100%	27 days	Mon 1/23/17	Tue 2/28/17	16	Project Manager 2, Project Team 2	Mon 4/25/16	Tue 2/28/17
25	1.1.2.3	Project 2 Closure Phase	100%	23 days	Wed 3/1/17	Fri 3/31/17	20	Project Manager 2, Project Team 2	Mon 5/30/16	Fri 3/31/17
27	1.2	Project 3: Implement Projects 1 and 2	100%	130 days	Mon 4/3/17	Fri 9/29/17	15, 3		Fri 7/1/16	Fri 9/29/17
28	1.2.1	Project 3 Definition Phase	100%	20 days	Mon 4/3/17	Fri 4/28/17		Project Manager 3, Call Center Directors, Project Team 3	Fri 7/1/16	Fri 4/28/17
32	1.2.2	Project 3 Benefits Delivery Phase	100%	89 days	Mon 5/1/17	Thu 8/31/17	28	Project Manager 3, Call Center Directors, Project Team 3	Mon 8/1/16	Thu 8/31/17
37	1.2.3	Project 3 Closure Phase	100%	21 days	Fri 9/1/17	Fri 9/29/17	32	Project Manager 3, Call Center Directors, Project Team 3	Thu 12/1/16	Fri 9/29/17
39	1.3	Program Operational Management	100%	260 days?	Mon 10/3/16	Fri 9/29/17			Fri 1/1/16	Fri 9/29/17
40	1.3.1	Program Operational Management Definition	100%	21 days?	Mon 10/3/16	Mon 10/31/16		Program Manager	Fri 1/1/16	Mon 10/31/16
44	1.3.2	Program Operational Management Benefits Delivery Phase	100%	199 days?	Tue 11/1/16	Fri 8/4/17	40	Program Manager	Mon 2/1/16	Fri 8/4/17
49	1.3.3	Program Operational Management Closure Phase	100%	40 days?	Mon 8/7/17	Fri 9/29/17	44	Program Manager	Fri 1/1/16	Fri 9/29/17

Figure 8-4:   The program management plan is complete and closed during the program closure phase.

dates to identify tasks that started and finished later than scheduled. A program manager also runs reports to review with the program governance board and receives approval for program closure.

Program Closure Phase

During the program closure phase, a program manager marks all program tasks as 100% complete. A program manager analyzes program actual start and finish dates, compares them with the scheduled start and finish dates to identify tasks that started and finished later than scheduled, and runs a series of program reports. A program management plan, along with other program artifacts, is transitioned to the ongoing operations.

Program Monitoring and Periodic Evaluation

Program monitoring and periodic evaluation ensure successful program execution. It ensures that a program delivers all benefits, and is being executed on time and within budget. Program monitoring and periodic evaluation take place on both the program and component levels.

Program monitoring and periodic evaluation take place during the entire program life cycle with different steps being executed during each phase. During the program definition phase, a program manager plans program monitoring and periodic evaluation of a program and its components. During the program benefits delivery phase, a program manager executes program monitoring and periodic evaluation. The execution occurs on the component level with oversight on the program level. During the program closure phase, a program manager closes program monitoring and periodic evaluation. The closure occurs on the component level with oversight on the program level.

Program Definition Phase

During the program definition phase, a program manager develops a program monitoring plan. The plan defines how the program execution will be monitored and evaluated. Objectives of the program monitoring and evaluation may include ensuring that a program is on track to deliver all benefits, is executed on time and on budget, there is no duplicate work, there are no gaps in work, and resources are used as planned. Program monitoring may utilize various techniques, including phase-gate review, program audit, program deep dive, and a readiness review.

Phase gate is a review at the end of a phase in which a decision is made to continue to the next phase, to continue with modification, or to end a project or a program.[28] Phase gate has three main objectives: ensures the quality of program execution, confirms the validity of business rationale behind program execution, and confirms program management plans and resources requests. A program manager authorizes a phase-gate review team, which includes selected members of the program team and a program governance board, develops a phase-gate review template, and determines phase-gate review frequency.

A *program audit* is a process of inspecting a program, which can be performed internally by a designee within a program, by an audit department, or externally by a government agency. Program audit objectives may include an assurance that a program is being executed as planned, meets program quality standards, attests to the regulatory requirements, and meets industry standards.

A *program deep dive* includes a detailed program and component review. Program deep dive objectives may include program scope validation, program interdependencies identification, and program risk mitigation planning. A program manager forms the deep-dive team, develops the deep-dive checklist, and determines deep-dive frequency.

A *readiness review* includes all activities that need to be completed before a program or a component delivers benefits. A program manager appoints a readiness review committee, develops a readiness checklist, and determines readiness review frequency.

Program Benefits Delivery Phase

During the program benefits delivery phase, a program manager executes a program monitoring plan, which utilizes techniques defined in the program monitoring plan, including phase-gate review, program audit, program deep dive, and a readiness review. A program manager executes each technique with the frequency described in the program monitoring plan. An exception to this rule is an external audit, where a government agency determines audit content and frequency. A program manager updates a program sponsor and a program governance board of the results of the program monitoring plan execution.

---

[28] PMI. (2015). *PMI lexicon of project management terms, Version 3.0*. Newtown Square, PA: Author.

Program Closure Phase

During the program closure phase, a program manager finishes a program monitoring plan. A final plan states if a program delivered all benefits, was executed on time and on budget, did not have any duplicate work, did not have gaps in work, and used resources as planned. A program manager delivers the final plan to the program sponsor and the program governance board.

Program Risk Management

All programs encounter risks! A *program risk* is an event or series of events or conditions that, if they occur, may affect the success of the program. Positive risks are often referred to as opportunities and negative risks as threats. These risks arise from the program components and their interactions with each other—from technical complexity, schedule, and cost constraints—and with the broader environment in which the program is managed.

It is essential to define risk profiles of organizations to construct the most suitable approach to managing program risks, adjusting risk sensitivity, and monitoring risk criticality. Risk targets and risk thresholds influence the program management plan.[29] A risk profile includes risk categorization into high, medium, and low, which can be done based on assessing the level of impact on a program and a component, and a probability of occurrence.

High, medium, and low risks have a different level of impact on a program and a component:

- *High risk* can significantly impact a program or a component's cost, schedule, or performance;
- *Medium risk* can somewhat impact a program or a component's cost, schedule, or performance; and
- *Low risk* can minimally impact a program or a component's cost, schedule, or performance.

---

[29] PMI. (2013). *The standard for program management* – Third edition. Newtown Square, PA: Author.

High, medium, and low risks have a different probability of occurrence:

- High risk has 70% or higher probability of occurrence;
- Medium risk has 30%–70% probability of occurrence;
- Low risk has 30% or lower probability of occurrence.

External and internal program factors can cause risks. External factors mostly cause program-level risks. Examples of external factors include political unrest, terrorist attacks, wars, tornadoes, and hurricanes. Internal factors can cause either program or component-level risks. Examples of internal factors that cause program-level risks include lack of system functionality, inefficient program initiation phase structure, and an absence of a program management tool. Examples of internal factors that cause component-level risks include resource constraints, changes to a component's scope, and delays with deliverables completion.

Organizations may have predefined approaches to risk management such as risk categories, the common definition of concepts and terms, risk statement formats, standard templates, roles and responsibilities, and authority levels for decision making. Lessons learned from executing similar programs in the past are also critical assets to be reviewed as a component of establishing an effective risk management plan.[30]

To have greater influence over the program, you give up direct control over each project task. The program manager is not a firefighter, but instead looks for changes or delays in activities, identifies possible risks, and prepares the team for things that could go wrong.[31] Risks can be encountered during all phases of the program life cycle. It is important to anticipate risks, as with time, their impact on a program may increase. Thus, it is critical for a successful program execution to identify, track, and mitigate risks.

---

[30] PMI. (2013). *The standard for program management* – Third edition. Newtown Square, PA: Author.
[31] Merrick, A. (2015). *Allied forces*. Retrieved from http://www.pmi.org/-/media/pmi/landing-pages/business-analysis-tools-silverpop/pdf/allied-forces-project-management-business-analysis.pdf

Program risk monitoring and control is the activity of identifying, analyzing, and planning of new risks; tracking identified risks and those on the watch list; and re-analyzing existing risks. Monitoring reduces the impact of a threat and maximizes the impact of an opportunity by identifying, analyzing, reporting, and managing risks on a continuous basis. Risk monitoring and control is an ongoing activity for the duration of the program.

The program manager identifies risks that can threaten the program's existence and develops a mitigation plan, such as environmental changes or governmental policies and regulations.[32]

Program Risk Management

Risk management is at the heart of project management. Any number of risks can befall a project and drive it off course, often through no fault of the project team. From hurricanes and political unrest, to supplier conflicts and labor shortages, internal and external events can have a significant impact on a project's progress and ultimate performance. Such risks are not fully predictable, but with effective risk management practices, potential damage can be mitigated.

Even though risk management practice is vital to successful program execution, in 2015 only 64% of organizations reported the frequent use of risk management practice, down from a high of 71% in 2012. While this number has declined, and is something that PMI will continue to monitor, the study does find that 83% of high performers report frequent use of risk management practices, compared to only 49% of low performers.

A risk management competency helps organizations assess and identify project risks, mitigate threats, and capitalize on opportunities. In fact, organizations that report they always use risk management practices have significantly better project outcomes compared to organizations that do not, as shown in Figure 8-5.[33] Figure 8-5 reports statistics

---

[32] Merrick, A. (2015). *Allied forces.* Retrieved from http://www.pmi.org/-/media/pmi/landing-pages/business-analysis-tools-silverpop/pdf/allied-forces-project-management-business-analysis.pdf

[33] PMI. (2015). *Pulse of the profession®: Capturing the value of project management.* Newtown Square, PA: Author.

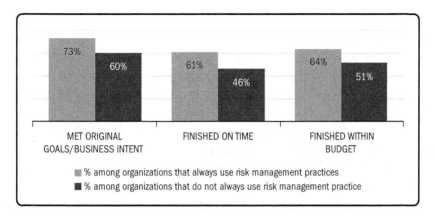

Figure 8-5:   Risk management and project outcomes.

for project management. Data on risk management and program outcomes are not available, so we assume that risk management and program outcomes have a similar correlation as risk management and project outcomes.

Program risk management occurs during all phases of the program life cycle. During the definition phase, a program manager performs program risk management planning. During the benefits delivery phase, a program manager identifies, registers, monitors, and mitigates risks. During the closure phase, a program manager closes all risks.

Program risk management planning identifies how to approach and conduct risk management activities for a program by considering its components. It occurs during the program definition phase. The risk management plan—the output of this activity—defines the approach to be used for managing risks.

Risk identification is an iterative activity that occurs during the benefits delivery phase. As the program progresses, new risks may evolve or become known. The frequency of iteration and involvement of participants may vary, but the format of the risk statements should be consistent. This allows for the comparison of risk events in the program. During risk identification, each program team member forecasts the outcomes of current strategies, plans, and activities, and exercises their best judgment to identify new risks. It is important to include contextual information that narrates how or why the risk may affect the program's success; the identification activity should provide sufficient information to allow the risk to be analyzed and prioritized.[34]

Risk monitoring involves tracking program-level risks identified in the program risk register and identifying new risks that emerge during the execution of the program, for example, unresolved component-level risks that demand resolution at the program level. Required actions may include determining if new risks have developed, current risks have changed, risks have been triggered, risk responses are in place where necessary and are effective, and program assumptions are still valid.[35]

There are many tools that allow tracking risks, including applications like Microsoft Office Project Server, SharePoint drive, homegrown software packages, and Excel spreadsheets. Microsoft Office Project Server, SharePoint drive, and similar applications have built-in functionality that allows registering risks and monitoring their resolutions. If applications are not available, a program manager can always build a risk register in Excel.

A risk register, which allows successfully registering, tracking, and mitigating risks, may include the following columns:

- ID column corresponds to risk orderly number.
- Date identified column displays a date when a risk was registered.
- Program or component column states if it is a program or a component risk.
- The title column provides risk name.
- The description column provides risk description.
- Probability column defines the percent probability of risk occurrence, which can be high, medium, or low.
- Impact column defines an impact that a risk will have on a component or a program, which can be high, medium, or low.
- Owner column lists a project manager responsible for risk resolution.
- The status column describes if a risk is open or closed.

---

[34] PMI. (2013). *The standard for program management* – Third edition. Newtown Square, PA: Author.
[35] PMI. (2013). *The standard for program management* – Third edition. Newtown Square, PA: Author.

- Escalated to a program column states if a risk is escalated to a program level.
- Mitigation strategy column describes a strategy to mitigate a risk.
- Target resolution date column shows a scheduled date to resolve a risk.
- Actual resolution date column shows an actual date a risk was resolved and closed.

We will use the call center's process improvement program example to illustrate issue identification, registering, and mitigation. It was determined that project two, decrease call response time, needs to include an additional scope. The additional scope is a research around call response time for different call types. This is a risk, as it has a negative impact on the project two time line. Subsequently, this risk has a negative impact on the call center's process improvement program execution time line. As this risk impacts program time line, project manager two escalates it to a program level.

A program manager and a project manager identify a mitigation plan that includes executing research around call response time for different call types in parallel with the subsequent tasks. Parallel tracking is possible, as a research department, and not a program team, will execute this task. A risk register for the call center's process improvement program is presented in Figure 8-6.

ID	Date Identified	Program or Component	Title	Description	Probability 3 - High 2 - Med 1 - Low	Impact 3 - High 2 - Med 1 - Low	Owner	Status: Open or Closed	Escalated to Program, Yes/No	Mitigation Strategy	Target Resolution Date	Actual Resolution Date
1	1/9/2017	Project 2: Decrease call response time	Additional scope for project 2 to conduct research.	Research around call response time for different call types. Impact to the component time line that subsequently impacts program execution time line.	3 - High	3 - High	Project Manager 2	Open	Yes	Execute this task in parallel with the subsequent tasks. Parallel tracking is possible, as this task is being executed by the Research Department and not a program team.	1/20/2017	

Figure 8-6: Call center's process improvement program risk register.

During the closure phase, a program manager conducts closure activities, including review and closure of all risks. A program manager archives risk documentation for future usage and transitions program benefits to operations.

Escalation Mechanism

As a program manager, I have learned to become more proactive in resolving conflict rather than reacting to the crisis. I think regarding escalation rather than reporting. Reporting only conveys the status of an issue; there's no obligation from the receivers to take action. Escalation gets the leadership team involved in solving the problem. From my experience, escalation can be considered complaining, so in the kick-off meeting for any project, I try to define when issues are escalated and to whom.[36]

Risks that require escalation include risks that impact more than one component within a program or the program as a whole. Examples of risks that require escalation include resource and inter-group conflicts, incorrect expectations about roles and responsibilities, and risks to key project indicators.

Program governance and escalation procedures should be in place to allow risk assessment for possible impact across the organization. The risk register is used in risk analysis and identification of risks that need to be escalated to senior leadership.

When risks remain unresolved, a program manager ensures that they are escalated progressively higher on the authority scale until a resolution is achieved. Risks are first escalated to a program manager. If a program manager does not have authority to resolve them, a program manager escalates risks to an executive sponsor and a program governance board.

There are several types of escalation to consider:

- Sometimes you need a yes or no answer to a critical question, such as scope expansion, which is beyond program manager authority;

---

[36] Merrick, A. (2015). *Allied forces*. Retrieved from http://www.pmi.org/-/media/pmi/landing-pages/business-analysis-tools-silverpop/pdf/allied-forces-project-management-business-analysis.pdf

- Conflicts may require mediation from someone at a higher level with a broader view of the project or program;
- An information-only escalation simply keeps management informed of potential issues that may arise and require their attention in the future;[37]
- Component-level risks that cannot be resolved by the project management team at the component level; and
- Component-level risks that could be managed more effectively at the program level because they affect more than one component or require a higher level of authority to be resolved.[38]

After determining that a risk should be escalated, a program manager determines the right time and identifies a correct person to escalate it to. Frequent escalation may be perceived by management as either a program manager's lack of competence or a high risk to project success. Rare escalation may result in missing critical issues or time for management to step in and facilitate the needed timely resolution.

A program manager needs to ask these questions to help decide whether it is time to escalate:

- Have you made a sincere attempt to reach an appropriate resolution, but have found that you are at a dead end?
- Is this an issue that your boss would expect you to handle or to escalate?
- Do you have all the appropriate know-how to make the decision, or does another subject matter expert or stakeholder need to be consulted?
- Can you approach these experts or stakeholders directly, or is escalation the only way to obtain their input?
- Have you exhausted all other options and any further delay could have a detrimental effect on the project outcome or deliverables?

---

[37] Karekar, H. (2014, April 14). *Escalation—Let's do it right!* Retrieved from https://www.projectmanagement.com/articles/283756/Escalation-Let-s-Do-it-Right
[38] PMI. (2013). *The standard for program management* – Third edition. Newtown Square, PA: Author.

Once a program manager has decided to escalate, it is important to do it in a mature and professional way. Here are six tips for effectively escalating problems with your project or on your project team:

- You need to determine the right person to escalate to. The immediate manager may not be the one to escalate to, especially in a matrix organization.
- Escalate to an appropriate level in the hierarchy in which there is someone empowered to make the decision or intervene. Going "too high" may result in your request being sent down to a lower-level employee.
- Provide a concise summary of the problem and also indicate where detailed information can be found. Do not assume that the people you are escalating to have the required background information.
- State explicitly what you need. Don't leave any ambiguity. Make sure you say when you need it and the impact or consequences if the expected action is not taken in time.
- Follow up, even after sending that email and making the telephone call—do not assume that when you escalate, the ball is now in the other person's court.
- Use appropriate, respectful content. Harsh emails and telephone calls complicate more things than they solve.[39]

It is very important to define and document what risks should be escalated, what is the timing to escalate, and who are the senior executives to escalate to. If a risk escalation process is not defined and documented, it may result in erroneous, missed, or untimely risk escalation. If an organization does not have a risk escalation process, it is critical that a program manager develops one for a program.

Program Change Control Process

All programs encounter changes. Examples of program changes include changes to scope, schedule, budget, documents, and deliverables.

---

[39] Karekar, H. (2014, April 14). *Escalation—Let's do it right!* Retrieved from https://www.projectmanagement.com/articles/283756/Escalation-Let-s-Do-it-Right

Changes to scope include an increase or reduction in the originally defined scope. An increase in scope occurs when a need for additional scope is identified. Similarly, a reduction in scope occurs when it is confirmed that a part of the scope is no longer needed.

Changes to the schedule include changes to task start and finish dates. Changes to task start dates occur when a task can start earlier or later than scheduled. A task starts earlier than scheduled due to an earlier completion of a preceding task or resource availability. A task starts later than scheduled due to a delay in completion of a preceding task or resource unavailability. Similarly, a change to task finish dates occurs when a task can be completed earlier or later than scheduled. A task finishes earlier than scheduled due to fast-tracked work or availability of additional resources. A task finishes later than scheduled due to a delay in completion of work or resource constraints.

Changes to budget occur when a program needs additional funds or has unused funds. A need for additional funds occurs due to an increase in scope, a need to engage additional resources, a delay in schedule, or a shift in work to an earlier date. A program has unused funds due to a reduction in scope, a need to free up resources, an advancement of schedule, or a shift in work to a later date. Changes to documents and deliverables occur due to a change in scope, a need for additional content, and a request for edits.

Changes are caused by both internal and external program factors. Examples of internal factors include resource constraints, budget constraints, and a discovery of additional information that may alter program baseline plans. Examples of external factors include changes in regulatory requirements, changes in industry standards, and an introduction of new products and technology to the market.

We will use the call center's process improvement program to provide an example of change. During the benefits delivery phase, it was discovered that project two, decrease call response time, needs additional research around call response time for different call types. This is an example of an additional component's scope that was not known during the definition phase. It is caused by an internal factor, an identification of a need for additional research. The research department will conduct research. Thus, this change results in an increase to budget to pay for a research department resource.

Critical to project management is the establishment of a baseline from which to effectively execute a program. Any change introduced is normally tightly controlled with a penchant for change avoidance to prevent rework and drive assurance of the scope and time line. Critical to program management, however, is awareness of change occurring in the business environment, which will affect the success of the program. Program managers must be adept at navigating change and understanding the impact of change on the business goals driving a program.[40]

Change control is a process whereby modifications to documents, deliverables, or baselines associated with the project are identified, documented, approved, or rejected.[41] During the definition phase, a program manager locks program scope and baselines the program management plan by locking the originally approved tasks and their start and finish dates. A program manager defines documents and deliverables that will be produced throughout the program life cycle and gets approval for a program budget.

During the program life cycle, there may be changes to the originally approved scope, schedule, budget, documents, and deliverables. These changes require change requests. A *change request* is a formal proposal to modify any document, deliverable, or a baseline.[42] To process program change requests, a program manager establishes a program change control process.

Change Control Process

Program change control is a process whereby modifications to documents, deliverables, or baselines associated with the project are identified, documented, approved, or rejected.[43] A change control process is utilized during the program life cycle. During the program definition phase, a change control process is developed at the program level. During the benefits delivery phase, it is executed at the component level with oversight on the program level. During the program closure phase, a change control process is closed at the program level.

---

[40] Martinelli, R. J., Waddell, J. M., & Rahschulte, T. J. (2014). *Program management for improved business results*. (2nd ed.). Hoboken, NJ: John Wiley & Sons, Inc.

[41] PMI. (2015). *PMI lexicon of project management terms, Version 3.0*. Newtown Square, PA: Author.

[42] PMI. (2015). *PMI lexicon of project management terms, Version 3.0*. Newtown Square, PA: Author.

[43] PMI. (2015). *PMI lexicon of project management terms, Version 3.0*. Newtown Square, PA: Author.

Definition Phase

To process changes, a program manager establishes a program change control process. The process is established on a program level and executed at the component level with oversight on the program level. The process describes how to initiate, track, approve, implement, and close changes; it defines roles and responsibilities of all persons who participate in the change control process. The process may include the following:

- Define regular and fast-tracked change control processes, including timing of each step;
- Define roles and responsibilities, and establish approval thresholds;
- Develop change request process quality standards;
- Develop change request tracking mechanism and create change request repository tool; and
- Develop a change request form.

Change control process execution starts with the initiation of the change request form. As was defined earlier, a *change request form* is a document that outlines changes to the original program scope, time line, or funding, providing justification to help determine proper action. A change request is declarative; it states what change should be implemented, but leaves out details on how to implement it. A change request form can be a standardized functionality built into a Microsoft Office Project Server or a program's SharePoint site. It can also be a homegrown document developed within a program or by an organization in Microsoft Word or Excel.

During the definition phase, a program manager develops a change request form. During the entire program life cycle, component project managers and the program manager use the form to request changes. Depending on the nature of a program, organization and industry standards, and regulatory requirements, a change request form may include these fields:

- Change header that includes a program name and a serial number;
- Change title;
- Date a change request was created;

- Name and title of a person who created a change request;
- Change request status, open or closed;
- Detailed description of change;
- Change-supporting documentation, including technical specifications, data analysis, process flows, and more;
- Change impact on schedule and budget, including timing needed and funds required to implement change;
- Change start and implementation dates; and
- Approval status, approved or denied.

Large scope programs may have a change manager. A change manager performs functions related to the change control process, including receiving a change request form, assigning a serial number, storing it on the shared site or drive, conducting an initial review, and taking it to the change control board and steering committee for review and approval. If a program does not have a change manager, likely a program manager performs this function.

After a change request form is created, it is submitted to a program manager or a change manager for processing and an initial review. Once submitted, a change request is assigned a serial number that allows tracking it throughout the change control process as well as to reference it at a later phase of the program or by other programs.

It is important to store and track change requests. If a change request is created in Microsoft Office Project Server or a program SharePoint site, it is tracked there utilizing a built-in tracking mechanism. If a change request is created in Microsoft Word or Excel, the file is stored on a program SharePoint site or a program's shared drive. A change request log, a separate document, serves as a tracking mechanism.

A program manager or change manager conducts an initial review of a change request. The objective for an initial review is to confirm that a requested change meets program objectives, and includes all necessary supporting documentation. The outcome of the review is either a recommendation for a change request to go through a change control process, a request for additional information, or a conclusion that change is not needed for successful program benefits delivery.

After an initial review, a change request is submitted for a formal review and approval. An objective of the change request review is to determine if a change is needed for successful program benefits delivery, it meets regulatory requirements and industry standards, and change cost corresponds to the benefit that will be realized by implementing it. Change request approval is usually set based on approvers' thresholds. Organizations grant approving power to individuals and committees within defined thresholds. Based on the thresholds that a change request falls into, an individual or a committee approves a change request. For example, a program manager may have the power to approve change requests for under US$10,000. A change request board may have the power to approve change requests within a range of US$11,000 and US$50,000. A change request steering committee may have the power to approve change requests within a range of US$51,000 to US$250,000. Organizational authorities, such as a capital approval committee or a CFO may have the power to approve change requests of over US$251,000.

Based on the organizational guidelines around approving power, a program manager establishes program thresholds and identifies people and committees that can grant approvals for each threshold. A program manager may establish a change control board to review and approve change requests for low and medium costs, and a steering committee to review and approve change requests with high costs. An outcome of the review can be either an approval or a denial of a change request. If a change request is approved, it will be implemented. If a change request is denied, it may be resubmitted with additional information that substantiates the request.

A *change control board* (CCB) is a formally chartered group responsible for reviewing, evaluating, approving, delaying, or rejecting changes to the project, and for recording and communicating such decisions.[44] A change control board may include a program manager, program team members, subject matter experts, members of the CFO team, and business owners.

A *program steering committee* is a committee that plays an important role in directing a program throughout program life cycle execution. It plans various functions, including monitoring program execution and budget spending, conducting phase-gate reviews, reviewing and approving change requests, and ensuring successful delivery of program

---

[44] PMI. (2015). *PMI lexicon of project management terms, Version 3.0.* Newtown Square, PA: Author.

benefits. A program steering committee may include a program manager, senior program team members, senior-level subject matter experts, CFO, and executive-level business owners.

A program manager establishes duration for each step within a change control process. For example, an initial review by a program manager or a change manager should be completed within two days of the change request submission. Change control board meetings should be regularly scheduled (e.g., biweekly or monthly to ensure timely processing of all change requests). Similarly, steering committee meetings should also be scheduled regularly (e.g., monthly).

A program manager defines regular and fast-tracked change control processes. If a change is not urgent in nature, it is processed through a regular change control process that includes all defined steps. If a change is urgent in nature, it is processed through a fast-tracked change control process that includes only critical steps.

A program manager establishes change control process quality standards that may include defining exceptions to the change control process, developing change request form standards, and determining the timing of change control process steps.

Benefits Delivery Phase

As stated earlier, change control process execution occurs during an entire program life cycle. The change control process starts with preparation, review, and approval of a change request. If approved, a change request is implemented. A component program manager monitors implementation and reports implementation status to a program manager or a change manager. If a change request implementation encounters issues, a component project manager resolves them or escalates them to a program manager where needed.

Once a change request is implemented, a component project manager reviews the outcome to ensure completeness. A component project manager closes a change request and reports closure to a program manager or a change manager.

Closure Phase

Change control process closure takes place at a program level. A program manager or a change manager confirms that all change requests were reviewed, and either approved or denied. A program manager or a change manager confirms that all approved change requests were implemented and confirms that all change requests were properly archived for future use by other programs.

Quality Control Process

Even projects that are delivered within budget and on time are not successful if the quality of the deliverable is poor. Quality management is all about identifying and following quality requirements, auditing the results of quality control measurements, and using quality measurements to control quality, recommending project changes if necessary.

Delivering high-quality benefits warrants on time and on budget benefits delivery and results in high customer satisfaction. In contrast, delivering low-quality benefits may result in missed delivery dates and the cost of rework. Quality is a variable cost for a program; it should be evaluated and incorporated into the business plan.

It is critical for successful benefits delivery to have a program quality management plan. *Quality management* ensures that a quality plan exists for overall program and project quality. The quality plan will also define program management metrics that will be used in providing early warnings of program failure points.

A quality management plan is used during the entire program life cycle. A program manager develops a plan during the program definition phase. A program manager and component managers execute the plan during the benefits delivery phase. The plan is cascaded down from a program level to the component level. A quality management plan is executed iteratively. A program manager closes a plan during the closure phase.

Quality management plan uses the program management plan, stakeholder register, and risk register as inputs. The program management plan provides the work breakdown structure, cost base, and scope baseline, including start and finish dates. The stakeholder register helps identify stakeholders that have an interest in and impact on quality. The risk register helps identify risks that may have an impact on quality.

The quality management plan includes quality standards, metrics, and measurement tools. Quality standards set up a framework of clear expectations around the quality of benefits that a program will deliver. Quality metrics are measurements that are used to compare benefits quality with the standards. Quality tools are used to measure benefits quality. Tools may include phase-gate reviews, internal and external quality audits, and documents review and approval processes.

Phase-gate reviews ensure benefits quality, as was described earlier. Phase-gate reviews are conducted at the end of each phase by a phase-gate review team that includes selected members of the program team and a governance board. A quality audit is a structured, independent process to determine if benefits meet quality standards, and meet internal and external regulatory requirements. Quality audits may be internal or external.

A department may conduct internal program audits within an organization or a project within a portfolio of which a program is a part. We will use the call center's process improvement program example. The program is a part of the call center's portfolio that has project one, call center's audit. The call center's audit is conducted for multiple purposes, including quality assurance of benefits delivered by the call center's process improvement program.

Government agencies conduct external program audits. External audits are especially important in the industries that have very high-quality standards, as they are directly responsible for human lives, including healthcare, aerospace, and car manufacturing.

Program documents review and approval is an important part of the quality assurance process. All program documents should be reviewed with the team that prepares the document, with the team that will use it in the next phase, and with executives. Review with the executives is a very important step in the quality assurance process, as they have a comprehensive view of the organization. Thus, through their review and approval of the document, the executives can ensure an overall cross-functional alignment. Among the reasons a program fails in quality is because executives do not take the time to review the documents, ensuring overall organizational alignment. An approach of using proxies in obtaining approvals may help with timing but, on the downside, may result in potential quality issues.

If any of the quality tools determine lower than desired benefits quality, it means that additional work is needed. In that case, a component project manager initiates a change request to conduct additional work to meet quality standards.

A program manager should balance quality of delivered benefits and program delivery on time and budget. If achieving quality results requires additional time, a program manager should evaluate various alternatives to ensure quality and secure on-time and on-budget delivery, including:

- Implement short-term solutions first and long-term solutions second;
- Implement manual solutions first and automated solutions second; and
- Conduct additional work needed to ensure benefits quality, then accelerate a subsequent phase by engaging additional resources.

Program Communication

In the context of organizational project and program management, communication is a core competency that, when properly executed, connects every member of a project team to a common set of strategies, goals, and actions. Unless project leads effectively share these components, and they are understood by stakeholders, project outcomes are jeopardized and budgets incur unnecessary risk.

The most crucial success factor in project management is effective communication to all stakeholders—a critical core competency to all organizations. In a complex and competitive business climate, organizations cannot afford to overlook this key element of project success and long-term profitability.

PMI research proves that ineffective communication leads to fewer successful projects; organizations that are minimally effective communicators report significantly fewer projects that meet original goals, come in on time, and complete within budget, as shown in Figure 8-7. [45]

It is critical for a successful benefits delivery to have a program communication management plan. *Communication planning* is the activity of determining the information and communication needs of the program stakeholders based on who needs what information, when they need it, how it will be given to them, and by whom.[46]

---

[45] PMI. (2013). *Pulse of the profession®: In-depth report—The high cost of low performance: The essential role of communication.* Newtown Square, PA: Author.
[46] PMI. (2013). *The standard for program management – Third edition.* Newtown Square, PA: Author.

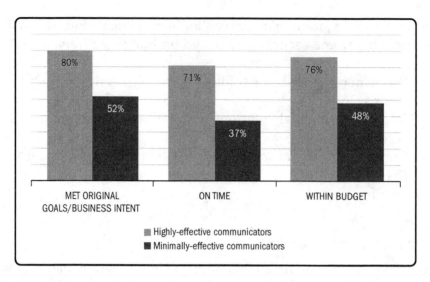

Figure 8-7: Organizations that communicate more effectively have more successful projects.

A communication management plan is used during the entire program life cycle. A program manager develops a plan during the program definition phase. A program manager and component managers execute the plan during the benefits delivery phase and close the plan during the closure phase.

Program communication can be internal and external. Examples of internal communication include communication to a program team, departments within the organization, program governance board, and executives. Examples of external communication include communication to the government agencies, external auditors, competitors, and suppliers.

A communication management plan describes communication protocols for various types of program communication, both internal and external. The plan needs to address stakeholders' needs and expectations, and to provide key messages in a timely fashion and format designed specifically for the target audience. Communication messages include program and component status updates, risks communication, change requests updates, budget information, external filings with the government, announcements, and press releases.

The program manager is the key communicator for the program. It is beneficial for the program manager to have a defined and documented strategy for the wide spectrum of communication requirements. This communication strategy is used throughout the duration of the program even if it is used as a quick reference to ensure that the appropriate message is delivered to the correct audience. This communication strategy should be updated regularly, as audiences and messages change throughout the course of a program.[47]

To ensure successful communication, a program manager needs to have strong communication skills. A program manager needs to be able to communicate up, down, and across with stakeholders, sponsors, customers, vendors, executives, and other program stakeholders. To communicate effectively, a program manager needs to be able to craft messages that will reach the targeted audience.

---

[47] PMI. (2013). *The standard for program management* – Third edition. Newtown Square, PA: Author.

CHAPTER 9

Effective Program Management

A program manager monitors program execution during the entire program life cycle and ensures program benefits delivery on time and on budget as well as ensures effective resource management. This chapter describes, in detail, activities and tools that can be used to deliver a program on time and describes the program financial management necessary to deliver it on a budget, including budget, forecast, and actual costs management during each phase of the program. Each calculation is illustrated with examples of financial management tables and accompanied with detailed descriptions on how to construct them. The chapter concludes with effective resource management during each phase of the program, including resource forecasting, estimation, and actual tracking.

This chapter includes the following sections:

- Mechanisms to deliver a program on time;
- Mechanisms to deliver a program on budget; and
- Effective program resource management.

Mechanisms to Deliver a Program on Time

A program manager monitors program execution during the entire program life cycle to ensure on-time program benefits delivery. A program manager regularly updates the program management plan to have an accurate view of the current state and utilizes various mechanisms to monitor on-time program benefits delivery, identify risks related to delays in program execution, shift priorities among conflicting objectives, and select mechanisms that fast-track components' execution in case of delays.

Program and component reports are one of the key tools for timely program benefits delivery. Reports allow monitoring program and component progress, identify areas of risks, manage interdependencies, and provide status updates. Reports can also be used for program communication to various groups including a program governance board and a program team.

A program manager may utilize existing reports that are built into a system used for a program management plan, or may create new reports. Microsoft Project has an array of reports that can be accessed by clicking on the Report tab > View Reports > click on the report type > pick a specific report. Microsoft Project reports are grouped into five categories, including dashboard, resources, costs, in progress, and custom. Each report category contains multiple reports:

- Dashboard reports include burndown, cost overview, project overview, upcoming tasks, and work overview;
- Resource reports include over-allocated resources and resources overviews;
- Cost reports include cash flow, cost overruns, earned value reports, resource cost overviews, and task cost overviews;
- In-progress reports include critical tasks, late tasks, milestone reports, and slipping tasks; and
- Custom reports allow for creating customized reports.

A challenge that many organizations face today is that reports are project-centric, supporting information tracking on the component level and not information aggregation on the program level. This limitation occurs because organizations often lack tools to aggregate and track program-level information. Many systems have limited or no functionality for aggregating program-level reports from component reports, including status, resource utilization, and risk reports as well as time lines.

Activities related to delivering a program on time take place during each phase of the program life cycle.

Definition Phase

During the definition phase, a program manager verifies program scope, identifies and on-boards program resources, and sets up program and component reports and metrics that allow tracking and measuring on-time program execution. A program manager also identifies which program and component reports will be included in the program status updates to the program executive board and program team.

Benefits Delivery Phase

During the benefits delivery phase, a program manager finalizes program scope, closely monitors program execution on the component and program levels, and identifies and resolves program and component risks.

A key mechanism to deliver a program on time is to monitor component execution. This is done by managing the program management plan, including:

- Updating task percent complete;
- Comparing start dates with actual start dates and identifying variances, including actual start date ahead of, on time, or behind schedule;
- Comparing finish dates with actual finish dates and identifying variances, including actual finish date ahead of, on time, or behind schedule;
- Reviewing program time lines to identify tasks that are behind schedule; and
- Using program and component reports to track timely benefits delivery.

As described earlier, a program manager utilizes a wide set of reports, including work and resource overview reports that are shown in Figure 9-1. Work overview reports contain multiple graphs that display a component's execution progress, upcoming milestones, and tasks that are behind schedule.

A resources overview report contains multiple graphs and a table that shows work status, resources statistics, and program status (see Figure 9-2).

During program execution, it is unavoidable to encounter risks that impact on-time program delivery. We talked about risk identification,

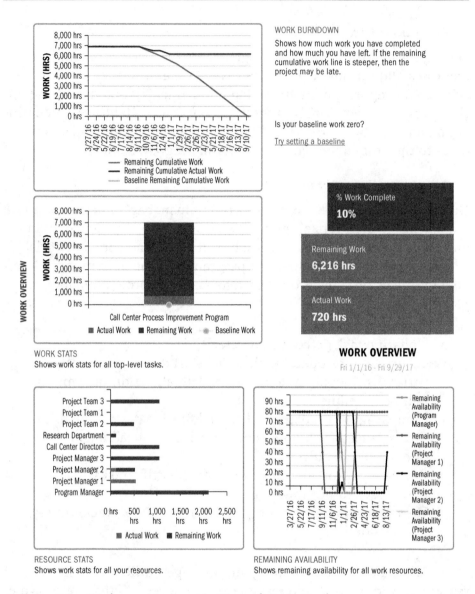

Figure 9-1:   Work overview report in Microsoft Project.

tracking, and resolution in Chapter 8: Program Management Infrastructure. In this section, we will focus on mechanisms that allow a program execution acceleration in case of risks that impact on-time benefits delivery.

If a program is experiencing a delay due to a component's execution actual time being longer than scheduled or due to a resource constraint,

RESOURCE OVERVIEW

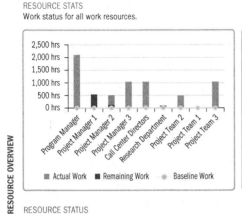
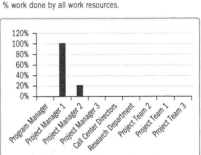

RESOURCE STATS
Work status for all work resources.

WORK STATS
% work done by all work resources.

RESOURCE STATUS
Remaining work for all work resources.

Name	Start	Finish	Remaining Work
Program Manager	Mon 10/3/16	Fri 9/29/17	2,080 hrs
Project Manager 1	Mon 10/3/16	Fri 12/30/16	0 hrs
Project Manager 2	Mon 1/2/17	Fri 3/31/17	400 hrs
Project Manager 3	Mon 4/3/17	Fri 9/29/17	1,040 hrs
Call Center Directors	Mon 4/3/17	Fri 9/29/17	1,040 hrs
Research Department	Mon 1/23/17	Fri 2/10/17	120 hrs
Project Team 2	Thu 1/19/17	Fri 3/31/17	496 hrs
Project Team 1	Fri 10/21/16	Fri 12/30/16	0 hrs
Project Team 3	Mon 4/3/17	Fri 9/29/17	1,040 hrs

Figure 9-2:   Resource overview reports in Microsoft Project.

there are various mechanisms to fast-track a program and to complete it within a baseline objective.

- Accelerate component execution by adding new resources;
- Outsource component work so that the partners can provide a solution quicker than in-house development;[1]
- Implement a short-term solution first and a long-term solution later;
- Implement a manual solution first and an automated solution later;

---

[1] Harisha Lakkavalli, PMP, PgMP, program management consultant and PgMP coach, Director at Avi Solar Energy pvt. Ltd.

- Use a phased approach to deliver benefits;
- Work in parallel on tasks that do not have interdependencies;
- Combine activities to fast-track program execution; and
- Reuse program documents and artifacts where possible.

If a component is behind schedule, one of the ways to accelerate component execution is to bring additional resources. This approach is effective, but may not be always visible due to budget constraints or resource unavailability.

Another effective mechanism to bring the component work back on track is to outsource the component's work so that the partners can provide a solution quicker than an in-house team. However, as in the previous case, this method may not be always visible due to budget constraints or partner resource constraints.

If, due to identified issues, delivering a full product or solution on time is not feasible, a program manager may identify an option of implementing a short-term solution first and a long-term solution later. Similarly, for the programs that deliver technical solutions, a program manager may identify implementing a manual solution first and an automated solution later.

A program manager may use a phased approach to benefits delivery. We will use the call center's process improvement program example. If there is a delay with component two, decrease call response time execution, then component one, improve call response quality, may be implemented first, and component two may be implemented later.

To accelerate delayed program execution, a program manager may identify tasks that do not have interdependencies and execute them in parallel. We will use the call center's process improvement program example. Component two, decrease call response time, can start earlier than scheduled, as it is not dependent on the completion of component one, improve call response quality.

To ensure on-time program execution, a program manager may identify, combine, and execute related activities together.

A program manager may identify similar documents and artifacts from the current program as well as from previously executed programs, and reuse them where possible. This approach ensures on-time program execution and avoids duplication of work.

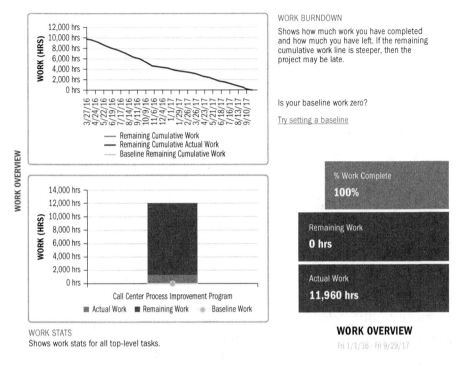

Figure 9-3:   Work overview final report in Microsoft Project.

Closure Phase

During the program closure phase, a program manager ensures that all benefits are delivered and transitioned, updates metrics to check if the program was executed on time, and runs reports, including a project overview report. This report contains a graph and a statistic that shows completion of program components as 100% complete (see Figure 9-3).

A program manager prepares a final status update on the program governance board and program team about on-time program execution. Lastly, a program manager closes a program.

Mechanisms to Deliver a Program on Budget

Program financial management includes the activities involved in identifying the program's financial sources and resources, integrating the budgets of the program components, developing the overall budget of the program, and controlling costs throughout the duration of both the components and the program.[2] It also includes developing and using program procedures for tracking, analyzing, and reporting program financials to the program sponsor, governance board, and stakeholders.

High program costs and potentially sizable use of the organizational budget result in different ways of estimating, authorizing, recording, and reporting program costs. Program costs are significantly higher than project costs for two main reasons:

- Programs are larger than projects and include multiple components; and
- Programs include more types of costs than projects include, for example, capital costs and program operational management costs.

Differently from project cost estimating, program cost estimating is iterative throughout the program life cycle. Program cost estimating is also more multifaceted, as it may utilize complex financial modeling. For example, weight or probability may be applied based on the risk and complexity of the work to be performed to derive a confidence factor in the estimate. This confidence factor is used to determine the potential range of program costs.[3] The responsibility associated with authorizing, recording, and reporting program costs involves senior organization leadership. In contrast, the responsibility associated with authorizing project costs resides with the project sponsor; the responsibility associated with recording and reporting project costs resides with a project manager.

The CFO is involved during strategy definition and initial program cost estimating. CFO engagement continues throughout the program life cycle with different responsibilities including a go/no-go funding decision at each stage of the program, periodic program cost reviews, and approvals to obtain additional or return unused funds. Often, the CFO performs these responsibilities as a member of a program governance board. The CFO's office may assist with financial modeling for program

---

[2] PMI. (2013). *The standard for program management* – Third edition. Newtown Square, PA: Author.

[3] PMI. (2013). *The standard for program management* – Third edition. Newtown Square, PA: Author.

cost estimating, variance analysis, and in preparing change requests to obtain or return funds.

In the subsequent sections, we will review program financial management steps that a program manager and a program team perform during each phase of the program life cycle.

Program Definition Phase

A program manager performs initial cost estimating during the program definition phase. When estimating program costs, decision makers need to consider not only the development and implementation costs, but also sustainment costs that may occur after program completion. Thus, total program cost includes program and sustainment costs. Total program cost represents the cost of benefits that a program will deliver. Program cost is compared with the costs of other programs to justify program selection and to determine if the organization has the appropriate funds.

Early in the definition phase, a program manager establishes a *program financial framework*. A program financial framework defines program funding flow, ensuring that the money is spent efficiently.

Program type and funding structure define the program's financial environment. Often, a program may be funded by one or more sources, and different sources may fund program components. Funding models include:

- Funding by a single organization;
- Managing by a single organization, but funding separately;
- Funding and managing entirely from outside the parent organization; and
- Supporting by internal and external funding sources.

In addition to funding sources, funding distribution has a direct impact on the program financial framework. Differently from projects, programs incur costs earlier than benefits delivery. A program financial framework ensures securing funding to bridge the gap between paying out program costs and delivering program benefits. Covering this large negative cash balance in the most effective way is a key challenge for a program financial framework.

As program funding requires large amounts, the funding organization is actively involved, and has inputs for the program management as well as requires regular updates on the fund's usage. Communication and updates with the funding organization should be regular throughout the life cycle of the program.[4]

Using a program financial framework, a program manager develops a program financial management plan. A *program financial management plan* is a component of the program management plan that documents all of the program financial aspects, including funding sources and distribution, financial metrics, financial reporting mechanisms, and an initial budget.

As a part of the program financial management plan, a program manager and a program team develop financial metrics that are used to measure program benefits. The program governance board validates financial metrics. As programs are usually large in scope and long in duration, a challenge around developing financial metrics is to establish a cause-and-effect relationship. As changes to cost, schedule, and scope occur throughout the program life cycle, costs are measured against a baseline. Decisions to continue a program, cancel it, or modify it are based, in part, on the results of these financial metrics.

Preliminary budget planning starts during the definition phase. The initial order of magnitude cost estimates, completed to obtain program funding, serve as a basis for a program budget. The *program budget* includes total program costs that are required to deliver program benefits. The program budget is estimated at the component level and consolidated at the program level.

Organizations may use various approaches to estimating program costs, including use of complex financial modeling. We will use a bottom-up approach to illustrate how to estimate a program budget. The *bottom-up budget approach* includes estimating component costs and consolidating them at the program level to calculate program budget. Program budget estimating uses a variety of financial information, including component costs, program operational management costs, and costs to transition a program to ongoing operations. It is important to note that the majority of the program costs are incurred by components and not by the program.

---

[4] PMI. (2013). *The standard for program management* – Third edition. Newtown Square, PA: Author.

The program budget serves as a baseline for program costs. It should include sufficient details about component costs so that the program costs can be tracked as part of the program budget baseline. A program manager develops mechanisms to deliver a program on budget. Mechanisms include tracking actual program costs, comparing them to budget and forecast, and calculating budget and forecast variances.

For accurate cost estimation, actual program costs should be tracked at the component level and at the unit level (e.g., resources, capital spending, fixed assets, and tangible assets). To track unit-level costs, organizations utilize systems and tools, including Microsoft Server, accounting systems, Excel spreadsheets, and an Access database.

A challenge that many organizations face today is that financial processes are project-centric and not program-centric (e.g., actuals are tracked, and the forecast is built at a component level). A project-centric approach to financial management places difficulties to program aggregation and limits program and component-level variance analyses. Thus, it is critical for program management to have a tool to aggregate component financials into program financials.

We will continue to use the call center's process improvement program example to illustrate a program budget calculation process. As previously mentioned, the call center process improvement program includes four components—project one, improve call response quality; project two, decrease call response time; project three, implement projects one and two in all call centers; and program operational management. Program budget calculation starts with estimating costs, durations, and start dates for each component:

- The cost of project one, improve call response quality, is US$65,000; project one starts on 3 October 2016 and has a duration of three months;
- The cost of project two, decrease call response time, is US$65,000; project two starts on 2 January 2017 and has a duration of three months;
- The cost of project three, implementing projects one and two in call centers, is US$145,000; project three starts on 3 April 2017 and has a duration of six months; and
- The cost of program operational management is US$208,000; program operational management starts on 3 October 2017 and has a duration of twelve months.

We will illustrate program budget, forecast, and actuals calculations using tables. Tables have the following structure:

- Column one catalogs the call center's process improvement program components;
- Column two records the components' total costs;
- Columns three through fourteen list monthly component budgets calculated using monthly component budget (MCB) formula;
- Row one defines table headers;
- Rows two through five list program components;
- Row six records program total and monthly budget as shown in budget, forecast, and actuals tables presented later in the section; and
- Row seven records program quarterly budget, as shown in the budget, forecast, and actuals tables presented later in the section.

The program time line table lists all components, total budgets, and durations, as shown in Table 9-1.

Using total component cost and duration, we can calculate a *monthly component budget* as a quotient obtained by dividing the total components' cost by duration. This calculation assumes that the budget for all components is allocated evenly throughout each component's duration.

Table 9-1: Program time line.

Call Center's Process Improvement Program Components	Component's Total Budget (in US$)	Program Time Line											
		2016			2017								
		Oct	Nov	Dec	Jan	Feb	Mar	Apr	May	Jun	Jul	Aug	Sep
Project 1: Improve call response quality	$65,000	★											
Project 2: Decrease call response time	$65,000				★								
Project 3: Implement projects 1 and 2	$145,000							★					
Program Operational Management	$208,000	★											
	$483,000												

★ Denotes project start
Depicts project duration

Variables used in the monthly component budget calculations are defined as follows:

- MCB stands for monthly component budget;
- TC stands for total cost; and
- D stands for duration.

Monthly component budget is calculated using the following formula:

$$MCB = \frac{TC}{D}$$

To illustrate monthly component budget calculations, we will calculate a monthly component budget for project one. Project one has a budget of US$65,000 and a duration of three months. Project one's monthly component budget is equal to US$21,667, calculated as follows:

$$MCB = \frac{US\$65,000}{3} = US\$21,667$$

Similarly, using the monthly component budget formula, we can calculate monthly component budgets for all components, listed as follows:

- Project one's (improve call response quality) monthly component budget is equal to US$21,667;
- Project two's (decrease call response time) monthly component budget is equal to US$21,667;
- Project three's (implement projects one and two) monthly component budget is equal to US$24,167; and
- Program operational management's monthly component budget is equal to US$17,333.

Presented in Table 9-2 is a program budget table that lists all components, monthly component budgets, and durations.

Using a monthly component budget for all components, we can calculate monthly, quarterly, and total program budgets. The monthly program budget is calculated by adding the monthly component budget for all active components. For example, in January, the monthly program budget is equal to US$39,000. It is calculated by adding project one's monthly budget of US$21,667 and the program operational management's monthly budget of US$17,333.

Table 9-2:   Program budget.

Call Center's Process Improvement Program Components	Component's Total Budget (in US$)	Program Budget											
		2016			2017								
		Oct	Nov	Dec	Jan	Feb	Mar	Apr	May	Jun	Jul	Aug	Sep
Project 1: Improve call response quality	$65,000	$21,667	$21,667	$21,667									
Project 2: Decrease call response time	$65,000				$21,667	$21,667	$21,667						
Project 3: Implement projects 1 and 2	$145,000							$24,167	$24,167	$24,167	$24,167	$24,167	$24,167
Program Operational Management	$208,000	$17,333	$17,333	$17,333	$17,333	$17,333	$17,333	$17,333	$17,333	$17,333	$17,333	$17,333	$17,333
	$483,000	$39,000	$39,000	$39,000	$39,000	$39,000	$39,000	$41,500	$41,500	$41,500	$41,500	$41,500	$41,500
				$117,000			$117,000			$124,500			$124,500

The quarterly program budget is calculated by adding the quarterly component budget for all active components. For example, in quarter one, the program budget is calculated as a summary of program budgets for January, February, and March, and is equal to US$117,000. And last, the total program budget is calculated by adding the total monthly or quarterly component budget. For example, total program budget is calculated as a summary of monthly program budgets for January through December, or as a summary of program quarterly budgets, and is equal to US$483,000.

The monthly component budget formula assumes that the budget for all components is allocated evenly throughout a component's duration. This approach is not always accurate, as a component's work may not be executed steadily. There may be periods of more intense work with higher costs, and periods of slower work with lower costs. Unit-level tracking of actual costs helps account for cost variations. Unit cost details can be used to investigate budget and forecast variances and to develop mitigation plans. And unit-cost details can be used to justify additional funding requests.

During the definition phase, a program manager has limited information about program costs (e.g., not all components' costs may be identified). As programs typically have long durations, initial cost estimates need to be periodically updated. As more information becomes available during the benefits delivery phase, a program manager uses forecast to recalculate program costs more accurately, as will be described in the next section.

Program Benefits Delivery Phase

As the benefits delivery phase is iterative, a program manager periodically updates the program forecast using new information about component costs. *Program forecast* is a reoccurring process of estimating program future costs. Program forecast takes into account new information that becomes available throughout the program benefits delivery phase. An outcome of the program forecast is the *monthly component forecast cost*, an amount of money that is forecasted to be spent to deliver component benefits in a given month.

Program forecast frequency depends on program size, and it is a good practice to calculate program forecast as closely to the start of work as possible. Forecast for large programs should be performed weekly or biweekly, while the forecast for smaller programs should be performed monthly.

To illustrate the program forecast process, we will return to the call center's process improvement program example. Project two identified a need for an additional scope, research around call response time for different call types. A program manager estimates that the additional research requires 100 hours at a rate of US$100 and results in a US$10,000 increase in cost. Thus, project two's forecast increases to US$75,000, from an original budget of US$65,000. A program manager estimates that, similarly to budget, the forecast for project two should be allocated evenly throughout the duration of the project and confirms that the forecast for all other components remains the same. As the forecast for one of the components increased, total program forecast increased as well, as shown in the Table 9-3.

Table 9-3: Program budget and forecast.

Call Center's Process Improvement Program Components	Component's Total Budget and Forecast Cost (in US$)	Program Budget 2016			Program Forecast 2017								
		Oct	Nov	Dec	Jan	Feb	Mar	Apr	May	Jun	Jul	Aug	Sep
Project 1: Improve call response quality	$65,000	$21,667	$21,667	$21,667									
Project 2: Decrease call response time	$75,000				$25,000	$25,000	$25,000						
Project 3: Implement projects 1 and 2	$145,000							$24,167	$24,167	$24,167	$24,167	$24,167	$24,167
Program Operational Management	$208,000	$17,333	$17,333	$17,333	$17,333	$17,333	$17,333	$17,333	$17,333	$17,333	$17,333	$17,333	$17,333
	$493,000	$39,000	$39,000	$39,000	$42,333	$42,333	$42,333	$41,500	$41,500	$41,500	$41,500	$41,500	$41,500
				$117,000			$127,000			$124,500			$124,500

During the program benefits delivery phase, a program manager tracks components' actual costs on a monthly basis. *Program actuals tracking process* is a reoccurring process of obtaining actual program costs at the component level and for the program in total. *Monthly component actual cost* is an amount of money that was spent to deliver component benefits in a given month. Components' actual monthly costs are added up to calculate the program total actual monthly cost.

During this phase, a program manager's key responsibility is to ensure that actual program costs do not exceed program budget and forecast. A program manager tracks, monitors, and controls program funds and expenditures. A program governance board provides oversight to program funds and expenditures tracking, monitoring, and controls. Typical financial management activities include:

- Identifying factors that create changes to budget baseline;
- Monitoring environmental factors for potential impacts;
- Managing changes when they occur;
- Monitoring cost reallocation impacts and results between components;
- Monitoring contract expenditures to ensure the contracts disburse funds;
- Implementing earned value management, including budget and forecast variances calculations and analysis;
- Identifying impacts to the program components from overruns or underruns;
- Communicating changes to the financial baseline to the governance groups and the auditors, on both the program and component levels; and
- Managing the expenditures on program infrastructure to ensure costs are within expected parameters.

These activities are critical to ensuring that the program will deliver all benefits within the approved budget. A program manager uses *earned value management*, a program management technique for measuring program performance and progress in an objective manner. Program earned value management includes calculating budget and forecast variances that allow comparing actual program costs to budget and forecast.

Budget variance is the difference between program budget and actual costs. The budget variance is favorable when actual program costs are lower than budget; the budget variance is unfavorable when actual program costs are higher than budget.

Variables used in the budget variance calculation are defined as follows:

- BV stands for budget variance;
- PA stands for actual program costs; and
- PB stands for program budget.

Budget variance is calculated using this formula:

$$BV = \frac{PB - PA}{PB}$$

Forecast variance is the difference between program forecast and actual costs. The forecast variance is favorable when actual program costs are lower than forecast; the forecast variance is unfavorable when actual program costs are higher than forecast.

Variables used in the forecast variance calculation are defined as follows:

- FV stands for forecast variance;
- PA stands for actual program costs; and
- PF stands for program forecast.

Forecast variance is calculated using this formula:

$$FV = \frac{PF - PA}{PF}$$

Companies set up allowable ranges for budget and forecast variances, typically at $\pm$ 3% to $\pm$ 5%. Budget and forecast variances are calculated monthly as a part of the program's monthly financial process. For large programs, a comparison may be made as frequently as weekly. All variances should be justified, and may be subject to audit and program governance board oversight.

Using the call center's process improvement program, we will illustrate actual program costs tracking processes. The total budget of project one, improve call response quality, was US$65,000, with a monthly project budget of US$21,667. In January, project one's actual cost was equal to budget, and was US$21,667. In February and March, project

Table 9-4:   Program actual costs and forecast.

Call Center's Process Improvement Program Components	Component's Total Actual Costs and Forecast (in US$)	Program Actual Cost 2016			Program Forecast 2017								
		Oct	Nov	Dec	Jan	Feb	Mar	Apr	May	Jun	Jul	Aug	Sep
Project 1: Improve call response quality	$67,667	$21,667	$24,000	$22,000									
Project 2: Decrease call response time	$75,000				$25,000	$25,000	$25,000						
Project 3: Implement projects 1 and 2	$145,000							$24,167	$24,167	$24,167	$24,167	$24,167	$24,167
Program Operational Management	$208,000	$17,333	$17,333	$17,333	$17,333	$17,333	$17,333	$17,333	$17,333	$17,333	$17,333	$17,333	$17,333
	$495,667	$39,000	$41,333	$39,333	$42,333	$42,333	$42,333	$41,500	$41,500	$41,500	$41,500	$41,500	$41,500
				$119,667			$127,000			$124,500			$124,500

one's actual costs were higher than budget, and were US$24,000 and US$22,000 respectively. Thus, the actual total cost of project one was US$67,667, calculated as a sum of actual costs for January, February, and March, US$21,667, US$24,000, and US$22,000, as shown in Table 9-4.

The increase in project one's actual cost in February and March compared to the budget resulted in the negative budget variance of -4%, calculated using the budget variance formula.

$$BV = \frac{US\$65,000 - US\$67,667}{US\$65,000} = -4\%$$

As actual cost of one of the components increased, so did the program's total actual cost. The program budget for quarter one is US$117,000, while the actual program cost is US$119,667. This resulted in the program's negative budget variance of -2%, calculated using the budget variance formula.

$$BV = \frac{US\$117,000 - US\$119,667}{US\$117,000} = -2\%$$

If a program has a zero-budget variance, no further action is required. If a program has a positive or a negative budget variance, a more detailed analysis is required to determine reasons. Once the reasons for budget variance are determined, a program manager develops and implements a mitigation strategy to ensure program benefits delivery on budget.

If the forecast shows that a program requires additional funds, a program manager prepares a change request. A *change request* is a document that outlines changes to the original program scope, time line, or funding, and provides justification to help determine proper action. A change request to obtain additional funds lists additional benefits and weighs them against costs. Examples of change requests to obtain additional funds include resource rate increases, the addition of scope, and the addition of new resources. The CFO and the program governance body review change requests and determine proper actions. A significant increase in program costs may no longer satisfy the business case and may result in program cancellation. If the forecast shows that there are freed-up funds, a program manager works with the CFO to determine the use of the freed-up funds.

In the call center's process improvement program, the forecast for project two, decrease call response time, increased from US$65,000 to US$75,000, or by 15%. The justification for the increase is an addition of scope to research call response time for different call types. The research will require 100 hours of work at the rate of US$100. Using this information, a program manager prepares a change request for additional funding for US$10,000 and includes justification. A program manager presents a change request to the CFO and the program governance body for their review and determination of proper actions.

Program Closure Phase

During the program closure phase, a program manager performs the final financial analysis. The analysis includes a comparison of program actuals at completion with budget and forecast and calculation of final budget and forecast variances. If budget and forecast variances are equal to zero, a program manager does not take any further actions.

If budget and forecast variances are negative, program managers perform final analyses to explain the variances. If budget and forecast variances are positive, a program manager estimates unused funds and works with the CFO and the program governance board to determine the future use of freed-up funds.

Program final financial documents may be used to calculate the cost of sustaining program benefits and transitioning them to ongoing operations. A program manager stores all program final financial documents in the designated storage place (e.g., SharePoint site).

Effective Program Resource Management

Resource management allows for determining resource needs, acquiring resources, ensuring that resources deliver program benefits on time and meeting quality standards, and off-boarding resources upon program completion. Resource management ultimately allows executing a program on time and on budget.

Resource management at the program level is different than resource management at the component level; a program manager needs to work within the bounds of uncertainty and balance the needs of the components for which he or she is responsible. Program resource management ensures all required resources are made available to the project managers as necessary to enable their projects to deliver benefits for the program.[5]

Resource management occurs during the entire program life cycle and takes place on the program and component levels. Resource management starts during the definition phase, with resource planning taking place at the program level. It continues during the benefits delivery phase, with resource management taking place at the component level, and with resource prioritization and interdependency management taking place at the program level. Resource management concludes during the closure phase, with the resources off-boarding on the component level, and with oversight on the program level.

Program Definition Phase

Resource management starts with resource planning taking place at the program level. A program manager conducts *resource planning*, the activity of determining resource needs and timing when they are needed. Resource planning involves confirming existing resources and identifying a need for additional resources.

A program manager analyzes resource availability and understands resource allocation across components to ensure that they are not over-committed. Historical information may be used to determine the types of resources that were required for similar projects and programs.[6] A program manager collects data and conducts a detailed calculation to

---

[5] PMI. (2013). *The standard for program management* – Third edition. Newtown Square, PA: Author.

[6] PMI. (2013). *The standard for program management* – Third edition. Newtown Square, PA: Author.

estimate resource needs for the program, as will be described in the next section.

A program manager develops *resource requirements*, a document that outlines resource needs and defines roles that resources will play in a program and creates a *resource plan*, a document that includes resource estimates and records all information about resources, including roles they will play in a program, and when they are on-boarded and off-boarded. Once resource planning is completed, a program manager reviews it with the program governance board and obtains board approval.

Program Benefits Delivery Phase

Resource management is an iterative process that occurs during the program benefits delivery phase. Resource management takes place at the component level, with oversight at the program level. A component's project manager on-boards resources, monitors resources' daily work, ensures that resources execute their tasks on time, and produces and delivers quality documents. A component's project manager uses resource variance analysis to identify overutilized and underutilized resources, as will be described in the next section.

A program manager monitors resource usage at the program level, prioritizes resources, and manages resource interdependencies. *Resource prioritization* allows the program manager to prioritize critical resources that are not available in abundance and to optimize their use across all components within the program. During program execution, similar to the economics of supply and demand, the need for resources changes. The program manager manages resources at the program level and works with the components' project managers, who manage resources at the component level to balance the needs of the program with the availability of resources.

Resources are often shared among different components within a program, and the program manager should work to ensure that the interdependencies do not cause a delay in benefits delivery. It is achieved by carefully controlling the schedule for scarce resources. The program manager ensures resources are released for other programs when they are no longer necessary for the current program.[7]

---

[7] PMI. (2013). *The standard for program management* – Third edition. Newtown Square, PA: Author.

Program Closure Phase

Resource management completion takes place at the component level, with oversight at the program level. After all program benefits are realized, component project managers off-board resources. Component project managers also perform final variance analyses, comparing actual resource usage with what was budgeted, and determining if resource usage was as planned or had a positive or a negative variance, as will be discussed in the next section.

A program manager oversees resource off-boarding and ensures resources are transitioned to their future assignments. A program manager closes a resource plan and delivers it along with the final resource variance analysis results to the program governance board.

Resource Forecasting, Estimation, and Actual Tracking

Program resources estimation, forecast, and actual tracking, as well as resource constraint management, are fundamental processes that occur during the program life cycle. Next, we will examine, in detail, activities that take place in each phase of the program.

Program Definition Phase

Using the budget, a program manager calculates budget hours needed to complete work and estimates resource needs. Based on the calculation, a program manager defines resource roles and responsibilities and prepares a schedule. A program manager presents all of this to the executive sponsor and the program governance board for approval. After approval is received, a program manager acquires and on-boards resources.

Using the call center's process improvement program example, we will review the steps to calculate the program budget hours and resources. The call center's process improvement program includes four components:

- Project one, improve call response quality;
- Project two, decrease call response time;
- Implement projects one and two in all call centers; and
- Program operational management throughout the program life cycle.

Monthly component budget hours are calculated as a quotient between the monthly component budget and resource hourly rates.

Similar to monthly component budget calculations, this calculation assumes that hours for all components are allocated evenly throughout the component's duration.

Variables used in the monthly component budget hours calculations are defined as follows:

- MCBH stands for monthly component budget hours;
- MCB stands for monthly component budget, as defined in the previous section; and
- HR stands for resource hourly rates.

Monthly component budget hours are calculated using the following formula:

$$MCBH = \frac{MCB}{HR}$$

As calculated in the previous section, the monthly component budget for four components in the call center's process improvement program are:

- Project one's (improve call response quality) monthly component budget is US$21,667;
- Project two's (decrease call response time) monthly component budget is US$21,667;
- Implement projects one and two's monthly component budget is US$24,167; and
- Program operational management's monthly component budget is US$17,333.

For all calculations in this section, we will assume that all resources have an hourly rate of US$100.

To illustrate monthly component budget hours calculations, we will calculate project one's budget hours. Project one has a monthly budget of US$21,667. Using the monthly component budget hours formula, we calculate the monthly component budget hours equal to 217, as shown in the following calculation:

$$MCBH = \frac{US\$21,667}{US\$100} = 217 \ hours$$

Using the same monthly component budget hours formula, we will calculate monthly component budget hours for all components:

- Project one's (improve call response quality) monthly component budget hours are equal to 217;
- Project two's (decrease call response time) monthly component budget hours are equal to 217;
- Implementation of projects one and two's monthly component budget hours are equal to 242; and
- Program operational management's monthly component budget hours are equal to 173.

We will illustrate monthly component budget hours and program monthly, quarterly, and total hours calculations using Table 9-5. The table structure was described in the previous section.

Monthly program budget hours are calculated by adding monthly component budget hours for all active components. For example, in January, the monthly program budget hours are calculated by adding project one's 217 budget hours and program operational management's 173 budget hours, which equals 390 budget hours.

Quarterly program budget hours are calculated by adding quarterly component budget hours. For example, in quarter one, program budget hours are calculated as a summary of program budget hours for January, February, and March, and are equal to 117 budget hours. Lastly, total program budget hours are calculated by adding total monthly or quarterly component budget hours. For example, total program budget hours are

Table 9-5: Program and budget hours.

Call Center's Process Improvement Program Components	Component's Total Hours	Program Budget Hours											
		2016			2017								
		Oct	Nov	Dec	Jan	Feb	Mar	Apr	May	Jun	Jul	Aug	Sep
Project 1: Improve call response quality	650	217	217	217									
Project 2: Decrease call response time	650				217	217	217						
Project 3: Implement projects 1 and 2	1,400							242	242	242	242	242	242
Program Operational Management	2,080	173	173	173	173	173	173	173	173	173	173	173	173
	4,830	390	390	390	390	390	390	415	415	415	415	415	415
				1,170			1,170			1,245			1,245

calculated as a summary of program budget hours for January through December, or as a summary of program budget hours for quarters one through four, and are equal to 483 budget hours.

Using monthly component budget hours, we can calculate resources needed to deliver program benefits. *Monthly component budget resources* are calculated as a quotient between monthly component budget hours and working hours in a month. Similar to the monthly component budget hours calculation, this calculation assumes that resources for all components are allocated evenly throughout a component's duration.

Variables used in the monthly component budget resources calculations are defined as follows:

- MCBR stands for monthly component budget resources;
- MCBH stands for monthly component budget hours, as was defined earlier in this section; and
- WHM stands for working hours in a month.

Monthly component budget resources are calculated using the following formula:

$$MCBR = \frac{MCBH}{WHM}$$

For all calculations in this section, we will assume that there are 160 working hours in a month.

To illustrate monthly component budget resources calculations, we will calculate project one's budget resources. Project one has monthly budget hours equal to 217. Using the monthly component budget resources formula, we calculate project one's monthly component budget resources equal to 1.4, as shown in the following calculation:

$$MCBR = \frac{217}{160} = 1.4 \; resources$$

Using the monthly component budget hours formula, we will calculate monthly component budget resources for all components:

- Project one's (improve call response quality) monthly component budget resources are equal to 1.4;
- Project two's (decrease call response time) monthly component budget resources are equal to 1.4;

Table 9-6:   Program budget resources.[8]

Call Center's Process Improvement Program Components	Component's Total Resources	Program Budget Resources											
		2016			2017								
		Oct	Nov	Dec	Jan	Feb	Mar	Apr	May	Jun	Jul	Aug	Sep
Project 1: Improve call response quality	4.1	1.4	1.4	1.4									
Project 2: Decrease call response time	4.1				1.4	1.4	1.4						
Project 3: Implement projects 1 and 2	9.1							1.5	1.5	1.5	1.5	1.5	1.5
Program Operational Management	13.0	1.1	1.1	1.1	1.1	1.1	1.1	1.1	1.1	1.1	1.1	1.1	1.1
	30.2	2.4	2.4	2.4	2.4	2.4	2.4	2.6	2.6	2.6	2.6	2.6	2.6
				7.3			7.3			7.8			7.8

- Implementation of projects one and two's monthly component budget resources are equal to 1.5; and
- Program operational management's monthly component budget resources are equal to 1.1.

Presented in Table 9-6 is the program budget resources table that lists all monthly component budget resources and total program budget resources by month, quarter, and in total.

Program Benefits Delivery Phase

After completing the program forecast during the benefits delivery phase, a program manager calculates forecast hours and resources required. These calculations are more accurate, as they take into account the latest information, and they allow for optimizing resources allocation across the program. Frequently, programs exist in matrix organizations, where resources have dual or multiple reporting relationships. Thus, resources may have multiple responsibilities and conflicting priorities that a program manager needs to manage. We will examine resource constraints and discuss methods to address them in a later section.

Monthly component forecast hours are calculated as a quotient between monthly component forecast and resource hourly rates.

---

[8] Monthly, quarterly, and total program budget resources calculations were described in the previous section.

Variables used in the monthly component forecast hours calculations are defined as follows:

- MCFH stands for monthly component forecast hours;
- MCF stands for monthly component forecast cost; and
- HR stands for resource hourly rates.

Monthly component forecast hours are calculated using the following formula:

$$MCFH = \frac{MCF}{HR}$$

As calculated earlier, the monthly component forecasts for four components in the call center's process improvement program are:

- Project one's (improve call response quality) monthly component forecast is US$21,667;
- Project two's (decrease call response time) monthly component forecast is US$25,000;
- Implement projects one and two's monthly component forecast is US$24,167; and
- Program operational management's monthly component forecast is US$17,333.

We will continue to assume that all resources have an hourly rate of US$100.

To illustrate monthly component forecast hours calculations, we will calculate project two's forecast hours using the monthly component forecast hours formula:

$$MCFH = \frac{US\$25,000}{US\$100} = 250 \ hours$$

Monthly component forecast hours for components one and three, and program operational management is equal to budget, as shown in Table 9-7:

- Project one's (improve call response quality) monthly component forecast hours are equal to 217;
- Project two's (decrease call response time) monthly component forecast hours are equal to 250;

Table 9-7: Program budget and forecast hours.

Call Center's Process Improvement Program Components	Component's Total Hours	Program Budget Hours			Program Forecast Hours								
		2016			2017								
		Oct	Nov	Dec	Jan	Feb	Mar	Apr	May	Jun	Jul	Aug	Sep
Project 1: Improve call response quality	650	217	217	217									
Project 2: Decrease call response time	750				250	250	250						
Project 3: Implement projects 1 and 2	1,450							242	242	242	242	242	242
Program Operational Management	2,080	173	173	173	173	173	173	173	173	173	173	173	173
	4,930	390	390	390	423	423	423	415	415	415	415	415	415
				1,170			1,270			1,245			1,245

- Implement projects one and two's monthly component forecast hours are equal to 242; and
- Program operational management's monthly component forecast hours are equal to 173.

After calculating monthly component forecast hours, we can calculate monthly forecast resources. *Monthly component forecast resources are calculated as a quotient between monthly component forecast hours and working hours in a month.*

Variables used in the monthly component forecast resources calculations are defined as follows:

- MCFR stands for monthly component forecast resources;
- MCFH stands for monthly component forecast hours; and
- WHM stands for working hours in a month.

Monthly component forecast resources are calculated using the following formula:

$$MCFR = \frac{MCFH}{WHM}$$

We will continue to assume that there are 160 working hours in a month.

Component monthly forecast hours for project two are equal to 250. Using the monthly component forecast resources formula, project two's monthly component forecast resources are 1.6, as shown in the following calculation:

$$MCFR = \frac{250}{160} = 1.6 \; resources$$

Using the monthly component forecast resources formula, we calculated monthly component forecast resources for all components:

- Project one's (improve call response quality) monthly component budget resources are equal to 1.4;
- Project two's (decrease call response time) monthly component forecast resources are equal to 1.6;
- Implement projects one and two's monthly component forecast resources are equal to 1.5; and
- Program operational management's monthly component forecast resources are equal to 1.1.

Presented in Table 9-8 is the program forecast resources that list all monthly component forecast resources and total program forecast resources by month, quarter, and in total.

Using monthly component forecast hours and resources, we can calculate monthly, quarterly, and total program forecast hours and resources, as was described in the previous section and shown in the preceding tables.

Throughout the program benefits delivery phase, a program manager tracks program actual hours and resources. A program manager compares actual hours and resources to budget and forecast, calculates

Table 9-8: Program budget and forecast resources.

Call Center's Process Improvement Program Components	Component's Total Resources	Program Budget Resources			Program Forecast Resources								
		2016			2017								
		Oct	Nov	Dec	Jan	Feb	Mar	Apr	May	Jun	Jul	Aug	Sep
Project 1: Improve call response quality	4.1	1.4	1.4	1.4									
Project 2: Decrease call response time	4.7				1.6	1.6	1.6						
Project 3: Implement projects 1 and 2	9.1							1.5	1.5	1.5	1.5	1.5	1.5
Program Operational Management	13.0	1.1	1.1	1.1	1.1	1.1	1.1	1.1	1.1	1.1	1.1	1.1	1.1
	30.8	2.4	2.4	2.4	2.6	2.6	2.6	2.6	2.6	2.6	2.6	2.6	2.6
				7.3			7.9			7.8			7.8

budget and forecast variances that indicate variations in the program execution to the plan, investigates reasons for variances, and determines the risk mitigation plan.

Monthly component actual hours are calculated as a quotient between monthly component actual and resource hourly rates.

Variables used in the monthly component actual hours calculations are defined as follows:

- MCAH stands for monthly component actual hours;
- MCA stands for monthly component actual cost; and
- HR stands for resource hourly rates.

Monthly component actual hours are calculated using the following formula:

$$MCFR = \frac{MCA}{HR}$$

Project one's total budget was US$65,000, with a monthly project total budget of US$21,667. In January, project one's actual cost was equal to budget, and was US$21,667. In February and March, project one's actual costs were higher than budget, and were US$24,000 and US$22,000 respectively. Thus, the total actual cost of project one was US$67,667, calculated as a sum of actual costs for January, February, and March (US$21,667, US$24,000, and US$22,000).

Using the monthly component actual hours formula, we can calculate January's monthly component actual hours as follows:

$$MCAH = \frac{US\$21,667}{US\$100} = 217 \ hours$$

Project one's February and March actual hours are equal to 240 and 220, respectively, as shown in Table 9-9.

After calculating monthly component actual hours, we can calculate actual monthly resources. *Monthly component actual resources* are calculated as a quotient between monthly component actual hours and working hours in a month.

Variables used in the monthly component actual resources calculations are defined as follows:

- MCAR stands for monthly component actual resources;
- MCAH stands for monthly component actual hours; and
- WHM stands for working hours in a month.

Table 9-9: Program actual and forecast hours.

Call Center's Process Improvement Program Components	Component's Total Hours	Program Actual Hours			Program Forecast Hours								
		2016			2017								
		Oct	Nov	Dec	Jan	Feb	Mar	Apr	May	Jun	Jul	Aug	Sep
Project 1: Improve call response quality	677	217	240	220									
Project 2: Decrease call response time	750				250	250	250						
Project 3: Implement projects 1 and 2	1,450							242	242	242	242	242	242
Program Operational Management	2,080	173	173	173	173	173	173	173	173	173	173	173	173
	4,957	390	390	390	423	423	423	415	415	415	415	415	415
				1,197			1,270			1,245			1,245

Monthly component actual resources are calculated using the following formula:

$$MCAR = \frac{MCAH}{WHM}$$

Project one's monthly actual hours are equal to 250. Using the monthly component actual resources formula, project one's January monthly component forecast is 1.4, resources as shown in the following calculation:

$$MCFR = \frac{217}{160} = 1.4 \; resources$$

Project one's February and March actual resources are equal to 1.5 and 1.4 respectively, as shown in Table 9-10.

Table 9-10: Program actual and forecast resources.

Call Center's Process Improvement Program Components	Component's Total Resources	Program Actual Resources			Program Forecast Resources								
		2016			2017								
		Oct	Nov	Dec	Jan	Feb	Mar	Apr	May	Jun	Jul	Aug	Sep
Project 1: Improve call response quality	4.2	1.4	1.5	1.4									
Project 2: Decrease call response time	4.7				1.6	1.6	1.6						
Project 3: Implement projects 1 and 2	9.1							1.5	1.5	1.5	1.5	1.5	1.5
Program Operational Management	13.0	1.1	1.1	1.1	1.1	1.1	1.1	1.1	1.1	1.1	1.1	1.1	1.1
	31.0	2.4	2.6	2.5	2.6	2.6	2.6	2.6	2.6	2.6	2.6	2.6	2.6
				7.5			7.9			7.8			7.8

Using monthly component actual hours and resources, we can calculate monthly, quarterly, and total program actual hours and resources, as was described in the previous section.

After calculating the budget, forecast, and actual hours and resources, a program manager performs budget and forecast hours and resource variance analysis to understand if hours and resources usage is going as planned. Budget hours and resources and forecast hours and resource variances are calculated monthly as part of the program's monthly financial process. All variances should be justified, and may be subject to audit and program governance board oversight.

Budget hours variance is the difference between budget and actual hours. The budget hours variance is favorable when actual hours are lower than budget hours, and the budget hours variance is unfavorable when actual hours are higher than budget hours.

Variables used in the budget hours variance calculations are defined as follows:

- BHV stands for budget hours variance;
- AH stands for actual hours; and
- BH stands for budget hours.

Budget hours variance is calculated using the following formula:

$$BHV = BH - AH$$

For example, using the budget hours variance formula, we can calculate project two's budget variance hours in April as follows:

$$BHV = 217 - 250 = -33 \; hours$$

Project two's budget hours variance is negative, indicating an increase of 33 hours in forecast hours compared to budget hours.

Budget resources variance is the difference between budget and actual resources. The budget resources variance is favorable when actual resources are lower than budget resources, and the budget resources variance is unfavorable when actual resources are higher than budget resources.

Variables used in the budget resources variance calculations are defined as follows:

- BRV stands for budget resources variance;
- AR stands for actual resources; and
- BR stands for budget resources.

Budget resources variance is calculated using the following formula:

$$BRV = BR - AR$$

For example, using the budget resources variance formula, we will calculate project two's budget variance resources in April:

$$BRV = 1.4 - 1.6 = -0.2 \text{ resources}$$

Project two's budget resources variance is negative, indicating an increase of 0.2 in forecast resources to budget resources.

If a program has zero budget hours and resource variances, no further action is required. If a program has positive or negative hours and resource budget variances, a more detailed analysis is required to determine reasons. Once the reasons for budget hours and resource variances are determined, a program manager develops and implements a mitigation strategy to ensure program benefits are delivered on budget.

Forecast hours variance is the difference between forecast and actual hours. The forecast hours variance is favorable when actual hours are lower than forecast hours, and the forecast hours variance is unfavorable when actual costs are higher than forecast.

Variables used in the forecast hours variance calculations are defined as follows:

- FHV stands for forecast hours variance;
- AH stands for actual hours; and
- FH stands for forecast hours.

Forecast hours variance is calculated using the following formula:

$$FHV = FH - AH$$

For example, using the forecast hours variance formula, we can calculate project one's forecast variance hours in February as follows:

$$FHV = 217 - 240 = -23 \text{ hours}$$

Project one's forecast hours variance is negative, indicating an increase of 23 hours in forecast hours to budget hours.

Forecast resources variance is the difference between forecast and actual resources. The forecast resources variance is favorable when actual resources are lower than forecast resources, and the forecast resources variance is unfavorable when actual resources are higher than forecast resources.

Variables used in the forecast resources variance calculations are defined as follows:

- FRV stands for forecast resources variance;
- AR stands for actual resources; and
- FR stands for forecast resources.

Forecast resources variance is calculated using the following formula:

$$FRV = FR - AR$$

For example, using the forecast resources variance formula, we can calculate project one's forecast variance resources in February as follows:

$$FRV = 1.4 - 1.5 = -0.1 \text{ resources}$$

Project one's forecast resources variance is negative, indicating an increase of 0.1 in forecast resources to budget resources.

If a program has zero forecast hours and resource variances, no further action is required. If a program has positive or negative forecast hours and resource variances, a more detailed analysis is required to determine reasons. Once the reasons for forecast hours and resource variances are determined, a program manager either prepares a change request to acquire additional resources or works with the CFO and the program governance body to determine future assignments for off-boarded resources.

Program Closure Phase

During the program closure phase, a program manager transitions delivered benefits to the ongoing operations, off-boards resources, and performs final hours and resource analysis. The analysis includes a comparison of actual hours and resources at completion with budget and forecast hours and resources, and a calculation of final budget and forecast hours and resource variances. If budget and forecast hours and resource variances are equal to zero, a program manager does not need to take any further action.

If budget and forecast hours and resource variances are negative, a program manager performs final analyses to explain the variances. If budget and forecast hours and resource variances are positive, a program manager calculates unused funds and works with the CFO and the program governance board to determine the future use of freed-up funds.

Program final financial documents may be used to calculate the cost of sustaining program benefits and transitioning them to ongoing operations. A program manager stores all program final financial documents in a designated storage place (e.g., SharePoint site).

CHAPTER 10

Future of Program Management

In this chapter, we will discuss the future of the program management industry. To understand how the industry can grow and where it can improve, we will examine the current state of the program management industry, focusing on existing gaps. As the program management industry operates globally, we will discuss the global environment and future trends. Using the current state of the program management industry and future trends of the global environment, we will attempt to define the future state of the program management industry.

This chapter includes the following sections:

- Program management industry current state; and
- Program management industry future state.

Program Management Industry Current State

Currently, a very limited analysis is performed for the program management industry. Analysis for the program management industry is frequently included in the analysis of the project management industry. For example, the Project Management Institute publishes *Pulse of the Profession*®. The *Pulse* report is very much focused on the project management industry and has very limited analysis and data on the program management industry. We will use project management industry analysis and apply it to program management industry analysis to identify the program management industry's current gaps, as shown in Table 10-1. We will assume that project management industry trends are indicative of program management industry trends.

Table 10-1:   Program management industry's current gaps.

	Program Management Industry Gap	Project Management and Program Management Industry Statistics
Program Management Industry Growth and Maturity	The program management industry achieved limited growth in the U.S. and worldwide.	Currently, there are no statistics available to quantify the program management industry's current state and future growth in the U.S. and worldwide.
	The percentage of organizations with high program management maturity is low. The program management continuum shows that the organizational structure is varied highly, spanning from project-oriented to program-oriented.	The percentage of organizations with high project management maturity has not changed for the past six years. Program and portfolio management are equally established in organizations, with only one in six reporting the high maturity of each.[1] Program management maturity is reported at 40% in high-performing organizations and 8% in low-performing organizations.[2]
	Organizations have a limited understanding of program management value.	Just over half of organizations fully understand the value of project management, a number that has remained the same over the past five years.[3]
	Only a few organizations have high benefits realization maturity.	The percentage of organizations reporting high benefits realization maturity is at 17%, static from the past three years. And the percentage of organizations reporting low maturity in benefits realization is trending upward—nearly four in 10 now report low maturity.[4]
Program Strategy Alignment	Only a few organizations report program alignment with the organizational strategy.	Less than half of organizations report high alignment of projects to organizational strategy, a number that has been fairly constant for the past three years. Organizations also report that, compared to last year, fewer of their projects are strategic initiatives—that is, projects designed to achieve formulated strategy (an average of 48% of projects, down from 54% in 2015).[5]
	Not all organizations have program management offices, and those that do have them do not recognize the program management office's strategic role in aligning programs with the organizational strategy.	Organizations that align their enterprise-wide program management office to strategy report 27% more projects completed successfully and 42% fewer projects with scope creep. Less than half of organizations surveyed have an enterprise program management office and only 44% of those enterprise program management offices are highly aligned to the organization's strategy.[6]

[1] PMI. (2016). *Pulse of the profession®: The high cost of low performance—How will you improve business results?* Newtown Square, PA: Author.

[2] PMI. (2015). *Pulse of the profession®: Capturing the value of project management.* Newtown Square, PA: Author.

[3] PMI. (2016). *Pulse of the profession®: The high cost of low performance—How will you improve business results?* Newtown Square, PA: Author.

[4] PMI. (2016). *Pulse of the profession®: The high cost of low performance—How will you improve business results?* Newtown Square, PA: Author.

[5] PMI. (2016). *Pulse of the profession®: The high cost of low performance—How will you improve business results?* Newtown Square, PA: Author.

[6] PMI. (2016). *Pulse of the profession®: The high cost of low performance—How will you improve business results?* Newtown Square, PA: Author.

Table 10-1: *(Continued)*

	Program Management Industry Gap	Project Management and Program Management Industry Statistics
Program Strategy Alignment	In many organizations, executive sponsors are not effectively engaged with programs.	The average percentage of an organization's projects with active sponsors declined compared to last year: only 59% of projects on average have actively engaged executive sponsors.[7]
	Only a few organizations report program managers' talent management alignment with the organizational strategy.	High-performing organizations are more than twice as likely as their low-performing counterparts to align talent management to organizational strategy. [8] Due to a variation in the organizational structure, the program manager role spans from administration-focused to business-focused.
Program Management Industry Standardization	The program management industry is not standardized.	Nearly six out of 10 organizations use standardized project management practices throughout most or all of the enterprise. But only one in four uses standardized project management practices organization-wide, a decline of three percentage points from one year ago.[9]
	In many organizations, program manager proficiencies are not standardized.	On average, talent deficiencies significantly hamper 40% of strategy implementation efforts.[10] The percentage of organizations providing project management training on tools, competency development, and a defined career path remains unchanged since 2012. Just under half of the organizations report having a formal knowledge transfer process—a decline of 5% since last year.[11]
	Program management industry tools are not standardized and are project-centric.	Tools used in program management are not standardized within organizations and industry-wide. And the tools are frequently project-centric and not program-centric.
	Program management industry analysis is limited, and industry data vary significantly from source to source.	Program management industry data are frequently included in the project management industry data. For example, PMI's *Pulse of the Profession®* includes program management industry analysis with the project management industry analysis.
	The Program Management Professional (PgMP)® certification has a small spread, compared to the project management certification spread.	In February 2015, PMI reported only 1,200 active Program Management Professional (PgMP)® certification holders. In the same year, PMI reported 647,663 active Project Management Professional (PMP)® certification holders.[12]

---

[7] PMI. (2016). *Pulse of the profession®: The high cost of low performance—How will you improve business results?* Newtown Square, PA: Author.

[8] PMI. (2016). *Pulse of the profession®: The high cost of low performance—How will you improve business results?* Newtown Square, PA: Author.

[9] PMI. (2016). *Pulse of the profession®: The high cost of low performance—How will you improve business results?* Newtown Square, PA: Author.

[10] PMI. (2015). *Pulse of the profession®: Capturing the value of project management.* Newtown Square, PA: Author.

[11] PMI. (2016). *Pulse of the profession®: The high cost of low performance—How will you improve business results?* Newtown Square, PA: Author.

[12] PMI. (2015). *PMI-Certification-Overview-Kronos.pptx.* Newtown Square, PA: Author.

Program Management Industry Future

The program management industry operates globally. So, before examining what the future state of the industry will look like, we will discuss changes that the global business environment will likely have:

- Globalization will be taken to the next level, with more teams being dispersed and operating in the virtual environment;
- Advancement of technologies will continue at the accelerated rate, enabling instant connectivity and providing a platform for geographically dispersed teams;
- Deregulation will likely take place, removing barriers and allowing for easier and more efficient collaboration; and
- The agile approach will receive a wider spread in the program management industry.

The dynamic, rapidly changing, and complex business environment continues to emphasize the need for excellence in project, program, and portfolio management. A return to basics, embedding the project management mind set in organizational culture, could create a sustainable competitive advantage. An organization's ability to build and sustain its growth capacity depends on some critical factors, including having active executive sponsors on projects, establishing a well-aligned and effective program management office, and using consistent and standardized project management practices throughout the organization. Organizations continue to recognize the value of people who are versatile, have deep strategic insight, and who champion knowledge development and knowledge transfer as essential to performance improvement and competitive strength. Organizations need to embrace, value, and utilize project management—and both recognize and attribute their success to it.[13]

The program management industry's future state will be influenced by changes in the global business environment and shaped by closing current gaps in the industry. The program management industry's future state will likely include:

---

[13] PMI. (2015). *Pulse of the profession®: Capturing the value of project management.* Newtown Square, PA: Author.

- Program management industry growth and maturity:
  - The program management industry will grow in the United States and worldwide;
  - The number of organizations with high program management maturity will continue to grow, with more organizations operating as program-oriented;
  - The number of organizations that understand program management value will grow; and
  - Some organizations with high benefits realization maturity will grow.
- Program strategy alignment:
  - The number of programs that will be aligned with organizational strategy will grow;
  - An increased number of organizations will have a program management office and will recognize their strategic role in aligning programs with organizational strategy;
  - The number of organizations where executive sponsors are effectively engaged with the program will grow significantly, supporting program alignment with organizational strategy; and
  - Many organizations will align program manager talent management to the organizational strategy, consistently defining the program manager role as a business program manager.
- Program management industry standardization:
  - The program management industry will take significant steps toward standardization, including closure of current industry gaps;
  - In many organizations, program manager proficiencies will be standardized to the level of a business program manager;
  - Program management industry tools will be standardized and program-centric;
  - Program management industry analysis will be sufficient to understand industry trends, metrics will be standardized, and the program management industry will have its reports; and

○ The number of program managers with the Program Management Professional (PgMP)® certification will grow significantly in the United States and worldwide, contributing to program management industry standardization.

Increased complexity of the future competitive landscape will require a high velocity from the program management industry. To thrive in a fast-paced world and be able to respond to market changes quickly, organizations must create a culture of agility.

Successful organizations share a common feature; the ability to pivot and implement quickly to achieve competitive advantage. We define *organizational agility* as the ability to change or adapt rapidly in response to market conditions or other external factors, including new competitors, emerging technologies, customer demands, and sudden economic and sociopolitical shifts. The use of the agile/incremental/iterative tools and techniques of project management is vitally important in such scenarios, as they impact projects and programs, and the use of these tools and techniques is on the rise, according to PMI's 2015 *Pulse* report.[14]

Organizational agility requires effective communication and proper change and risk management. It can also include much more than the widely-used project management tools and techniques of agile and other approaches. In fact, agile approaches to project management and formal project management can—and do—co-exist successfully.

Project management is the application of knowledge, skills, tools, and techniques to project activities to meet project requirements. Agile allows teams to deliver projects piece by piece and make rapid adjustments as needed. Agile is not done in place of managing a project. Rather, it is frequently introduced as a way to speed up the phases of a project.

PMI's *Pulse of the Profession* findings indicate that the most important characteristics of an agile organization include flexibility and adaptability, open communication, openness to change, empowered team members, experiential learning, rapid decision making, and a strong customer focus.

---

[14] PMI. (2015). *Pulse of the profession®: Capturing the value of project management.* Newtown Square, PA: Author.

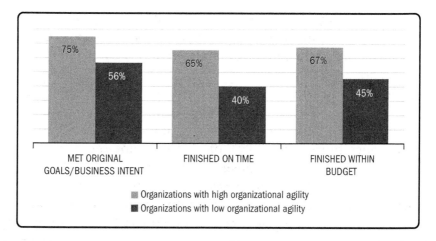

Figure 10-1:   Agility and project outcomes.

On their journey to becoming more agile, successful organizations overcome many barriers—including slow decision making, cultural mind sets that don't support agility, lack of executive engagement/ leadership, little communication between departments, and unclear organizational vision or strategy. These organizations overcome those obstacles by embodying the most important characteristics of organizational agility, such as:

- Flexibility and adaptability;
- Open communication;
- Receptive to change;
- Empowered team members;
- Experiential learning opportunities;
- Rapid decision making; and
- Strong customer focus.

What creates organizational agility? We have found some concrete leading practices at the core of success. They start with a firm grounding in the basics of project management, including an appreciation for the value of experienced and well-trained professionals and the standardized program management practices they use. Agile organizations actively engage executive sponsors, align projects to strategy, and establish a well-aligned and effective program management office. They also have better communicators, more collaboration, and more engagement. They are change enablers and manage risk effectively. It is the combination of all these elements that has led to their ability to adjust and adapt to rapidly changing market conditions.[15]

Highly agile organizations have significantly better project outcomes compared to low-agile organizations, as shown in Figure 10-1.

The use of agile/incremental/iterative practices in project management continues to rise, with 38% of organizations reporting frequent use, up eight percentage points since 2013.[16] It is expected that in the future state, the use of agile practices will continue to spread.

Program managers can influence the future state of the program management industry. One of the venues to help shape program management's current state is through the program management community of Practice (PgMCoP), as will be described in the next chapter.

---

[15] PMI. (2015). *Pulse of the profession®: Capturing the value of project management through organizational agility.* Newtown Square, PA: Author.

[16] PMI. (2015). *Pulse of the profession®: Capturing the value of project management.* Newtown Square, PA: Author.

CHAPTER 11

Program Management Community of Practice

A program manager needs to understand the organizational environment as it defines the program management structure and sculpts the program manager role. A program manager should influence business-focused program management structure as it empowers a business-focused program manager role. One of the venues that a program manager can utilize is a program management community of practice (PgMCoP). A community of practice can serve as a forum for program management's current state analysis, program process improvement initiative discussions, and best practice and knowledge sharing. This chapter defines the community of practice's value to organizations and program managers, and describes its foundation, structure, and operations.

The chapter covers the following key aspects:

- Program management community of practice value; and
- Foundation, benefits, structure, and operational activities.

Program Management Community of Practice Value

A *program management community of practice* (PgMCoP) is a forum that allows program managers to influence business program management structure, sculpt the program manager role, help standardize program management definitions, and share knowledge and best practices.

The community of practice can be either internal within the organization or external through networking sites like LinkedIn or professional associations like PMI. Even though as of January 2016, PMI members did not have local chapters for program management practitioners founded through PMI, this opportunity can be explored in the future.

The internal community of practice will allow program managers to realize the full spectrum of benefits within an organization, starting with influencing a business-focused program management structure. The external community of practice will create a platform for collecting knowledge and best practices that can be used to standardize and promote program management.

Foundation, Benefits, Structure, and Operational Activities of the Program Management Community of Practice

Foundation

Any program manager can find a program management community of practice. Organizations will likely support community of practice formation as they increase organizational performance in the following four areas:

- Help accelerate the on-boarding and learning of new program managers;
- Allow for responding more rapidly to customer needs and inquiries;
- Reduce rework and prevent "reinvention of the wheel"; and
- Spawn new ideas for products and services.[1]

A program manager can start the process of finding the program management community of practice by preparing and submitting a proposal to executives. The proposal identifies the need for the community of practice and justifies its foundation within the organization by listing future benefits. The proposal includes the community of practice structure, identifies program managers who will participate in it, defines lead and participant roles and responsibilities, and delineates executive oversight. The proposal outlines community of practice operations, including meetings cadence, frequency, and format of the updates to the executive sponsors.

---

[1] Community of practice. (n.d.). In *Wikipedia*. Retrieved from https://en.wikipedia.org/wiki/Community_of_practice

Various executives can be involved in review and approval of the proposal for the program management community of practice, including portfolio managers, program management office directors, and vice presidents of the functional areas that employ program managers. Once the executives review and approve the proposal, they appoint a sponsor, who will provide executive oversight and ensure community of practice organizational alignment.

Once approval is received, a community of practice lead conducts a kick-off meeting that includes program managers participating in the community of practice and an executive sponsor. A community of practice lead presents a community of practice structure, roles and responsibilities, and meeting cadence. Participants provide feedback that will help finalize the program management community of practice structure and meetings cadence. During the meeting, the lead obtains buy-in from the participants for a community of practice launch. A program manager schedules regular meetings and proceeds with the community of practice launch.

Benefits

It is important to fully define benefits that can be realized through the program management community of practice, as it confirms a need for the community of practice, justifies its formation to senior executives, motivates participants to take part in it, defines the community of practice goals, and informs the activity plan. In this section, we will introduce structural characteristics of the community of practice as it provides the framework for benefits definition. We will also examine benefits that a program management community of practice provides.

A community of practice provides benefits to three groups: participants, community, and organization. For the participants, the community of practice creates a supportive environment that promotes learning and professional development. It allows for interacting with professional peers, subject matter experts, and senior leadership far beyond the departmental walls. In more detail, benefits to the participants include:

- Broadening organizational awareness and understanding different roles within the organization;
- Expanding networks within the organization;
- Increasing recognition and enhancing professional reputation;
- Enhancing professional development and learning;

- Improving interaction with professional peers across the organization; and
- Increasing access to subject matter experts and senior leadership.

The community has the power to influence organizational decisions. It is also a platform for knowledge sharing and idea generation. Community benefits are generated from the benefits that the participants accumulate together, including:

- Power to influence organizational structure and decisions;
- Amplified idea generation; and
- A platform for knowledge sharing.

Organizations realize multiple benefits through communities of practice. The most tangible benefit to an organization is a business outcome, as the community of practice's benefits directly contribute to successful projects, process improvements, new businesses, and innovations. Organizational benefits include:

- Improved processes timing and efficiency;
- Improved delivery effectiveness; and
- Increased new businesses and innovations.

The structural characteristics of any community of practice are redefined to three domains: knowledge, a notion of community, and practice:

- A domain of knowledge creates common ground, inspires members to participate, guides their learning, and gives meaning to their actions.
- The notion of a community creates the social fabric for that learning. A strong community fosters interactions and encourages a willingness to share ideas.
- While the domain provides the general area of interest for the community, the practice is the specific focus around which the community develops, shares, and maintains its core of knowledge.[2]

---

[2] Community of practice. (n. d.). In *Wikipedia*. Retrieved from https://en.wikipedia.org/wiki/Community_of_practice

Using the community of practice's structural characteristic, we will examine program management community of practice benefits for participants, communities, and organizations, as presented in Table 11-1.

A program manager lead and program manager participants define the program management community of practice benefits. An executive sponsor approves benefits, ensuring overall organizational alignment.

Based on identified benefits, a program manager lead and program manager participants set program management community of practice goals and create an annual activity plan. The plan includes activities to be worked on and topics to be discussed during the year. For example, the program management community of practice sets an annual goal to standardize program governance structure across multiple programs. To achieve this goal, the activity plan will include a dialogue

Table 11-1:   Program management community of practice benefits.

#	Program Management Community of Practice Benefits	Community of Practice Domains		
		Knowledge	Notion of Community	Practice
1	Influence the organizational structure around program management.	✓	✓	✓
2	Shape business program manager role.	✓	✓	✓
3	Standardize program management and implement best practices.	✓	✓	✓
4	Identify gaps between program management's current and future states, and identify improvements needed to close the gaps.	✓	✓	✓
5	Identify gaps between the program manager role's current and future states, and identify improvements needed to close the gaps.	✓	✓	✓
6	Implement best practices either from external sources (e.g., program management industry) or from internal sources (e.g., different programs within the organization).	✓		✓
7	Share knowledge, program documentation, findings, and artifacts across multiple programs within the organization.	✓	✓	
8	Promote the quality delivery of programs and assist with developing and implementing program quality standards.	✓	✓	✓
9	Celebrate program successes.		✓	✓
10	Ensure organization-wide program management communication.		✓	

from each program manager to discuss their program governance structure, compare and contrast findings, identify gaps, and implement best practices. The activity plan is broken down into tasks that become topics for the program management community of practice meetings and may include:

- Identifying best practices;
- Advocating for a new system; and
- Identifying the need for an infrastructure enhancement.

The program management community of practice may use a template to collect findings through a dialogue with the program managers. The findings are analyzed to identify common program practices and gaps. Using findings, program managers make recommendations. Once approved, recommendations are implemented, improving program management practice.

Costs

Benefits generation is always associated with costs. For a community of practice, it may be difficult to quantify all costs and tie them back to the benefits, as there is a time gap between incurred costs and realized benefits. The community of practice costs may include the cost of participants' time, practice promotional materials, and technology.

The cost of participants' time can be quantified using hourly rates multiplied by the number of hours. Publishing costs can quantify the cost of promotional materials (e.g., cost to publish flyers that announce the community of practice events, and brochures that contain findings). The cost of technology can be quantified using hourly equipment cost. The community of practice meetings can be either in person or virtual. For an in-person meeting, technology cost can be a projector cost. For a virtual meeting, technology cost can be a video conference cost.

Structure

A program management community of practice should include the following roles (see Figure 11-1):

- *Program sponsor*, an executive who provides executive oversight and ensures organizational alignment;

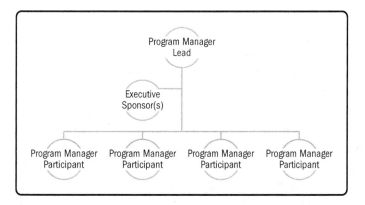

Figure 11-1: Program management community of practice organizational structure.

- *Program manager lead,* a program manager who leads the community of practice during a defined period; and
- *Program manager participants,* program managers who participate in the community of practice work.

As the community of practice is a volunteer organization where participants frequently deal with conflicting priorities, it is important to ensure participation utilizing these key steps:

- Clearly define the community of practice purpose, and ensure it accounts for all participants' needs;
- Justify participation by quantifying benefits; and
- Ensure portfolio manager and program management office director support.

Program manager participants can ensure community of practice success and can gain the most benefits out of participating in it by actively displaying the following three competencies:

- Social presence includes communicating with others in the community of practice. Lack of social presence may create barriers that inhibit individuals from engaging in knowledge exchange. Some of the reasons for these barriers include egos and personal attacks.

- Motivation to share knowledge is critical to the success of communities of practice. Studies show that members are motivated to become active participants in a community of practice when they view knowledge as meant for the public good, a moral obligation, and as a community interest. Members of a community of practice can also be motivated to participate by using methods such as tangible returns (promotion, raises, or bonuses), intangible returns (reputation, self-esteem), and community interest (exchange of practice-related knowledge, interaction).
- Collaboration is essential to ensuring that the community of practice thrives.[3]

What makes a community of practice succeed depends on the purpose and objective of the community as well as the interests and resources of the members of that community. Once the community of practice is operational, a program manager lead can take various actions to ensure its ongoing success, including:

- Designing the community to evolve naturally. As the nature of the community of practice is dynamic, the interests, goals, and members are subject to change. Community of practice forums should be designed to support shifts in focus.
- Creating opportunities for open dialogue with inside and outside perspectives. While the members and their knowledge are the community of practice's most valuable resource, it is also beneficial to look outside of the community of practice to understand the different possibilities for achieving their learning goals.
- Welcoming and allowing different levels of participation:
  - The core group, who participates intensely in the community through discussions and projects. This group typically takes on leadership roles in guiding the group.
  - The active group, who attends and participates regularly, but not to the level of the leaders.

---

[3] Community of practice. (n. d.). In *Wikipedia*. Retrieved from https://en.wikipedia.org/wiki/Community_of_practice

○ The peripheral group, who, while they are passive participants in the community, still learn from their level of involvement. The third group typically represents the majority of the community.

- Developing both public and private community spaces. While community of practices typically operate in public spaces where all members share, discuss, and explore ideas, they should also offer private exchanges. Different members of the community of practice could coordinate relationships among members and resources in an individualized approach based on specific needs.

- Focusing on the value of the community. The community of practice should create opportunities for participants to explicitly discuss the value and productivity of their participation in the group.

- Combining familiarity and excitement. The community of practices should offer expected learning opportunities as part of their structure, and opportunities for members to shape their learning experience together by brainstorming and examining the conventional and radical wisdom related to their topic.

- Finding and nurturing a regular rhythm for the community. The community of practice should coordinate a thriving cycle of activities and events that allow for the members to regularly meet, reflect, and evolve. The rhythm, or pace, should maintain an anticipated level of engagement to sustain the vibrancy of the community, yet not be so fast-paced that it becomes unwieldy and overwhelming in its intensity.[4]

As mentioned above, focus on the value of the community of practice is highly important. That is why one of the first community of practice meetings should include goal setting. For the first year, short-term goals may include developing the organizational structure and ensuring 80% meeting attendance. Long-term goals may include influencing program management business structure in three years and providing training to ensure business program manager role transition.

---

[4] Community of practice. (n. d.). In *Wikipedia*. Retrieved from https://en.wikipedia .org/wiki/Community_of_practice

To ensure outside perspectives, create new learning opportunities, and maintain excitement, the program manager lead, along with the executive sponsor, invites guest speakers. Among guest speakers may be industry experts; government officials; organizational, national, and regional program management executives; and personnel from various departments.

To maintain an anticipated level of engagement, the community of practice should have a set structure, including meetings cadence, as will be described in the next section.

Operational Activities

At the start of the community of practice, a program manager lead should set up the operational structure, including:

- Agreeing upon program manager lead duration of service;
- Scheduling community of practice meetings; and
- Scheduling updates with the executive sponsor.

Each year, the program management community of practice operations should start with the goal setting. The goals should include measures of successful completion. Examples of measures may include meeting attendance and goals completed to date. A program manager lead gains executive sponsor goal approval. And a program manager lead and the executive sponsor set up regular updates and agree upon update format.

A program manager lead sets up and maintains a document storage depository (e.g., a SharePoint site or a shared drive) and stores all program management community of practice artifacts, including meeting minutes, presentations, analyses, and more.

Glossary

*A Guide to the Project Management Body of Knowledge (PMBOK®
Guide)* is a set of standard terminology and guidelines (a body of knowledge) for project management.

Activity-based approach to building a program management plan uses tasks, duration, and cost from a similar program or a component.

Actual finish date is the date a task completed. A task may end on, ahead of, or later than the scheduled date.

Actual start date is the date a task started. A task may start on, ahead of, or later than the scheduled date.

Administrative-focused program management function is an administrative-focused organization that demonstrates a strong focus on independent projects and strong line-management control of projects.

Affected individuals or organizations are those who perceive that they will either benefit from or be disadvantaged by the program's activities.

Agility refers to an iterative, incremental approach to managing the design-and-build activities of engineering, information technology, and other business areas that aim to provide new product or service development in a highly flexible and interactive manner.

Alignment refers to the degree to which a program mirrors and supports the priorities of the organization's business strategy.

Annual strategic planning cycle is a process by which an organizational vision and mission are translated into a strategic plan within the boundaries of the organizational values.

Automatically scheduled tasks have start, finish, and duration values calculated by each project and are based on dependencies, constraints, calendars, and other factors.

Baseline is an approved version of a work product that can be changed using formal change control procedures and is used as the basis for comparison to actual results.

Benefits are outcomes of actions and behaviors that provides utility, value, or a positive change to the intended recipient.

Benefits analysis and planning institutes how benefits are realized and establishes how benefits realization is monitored by developing benefits metrics.

Benefits management on a program is the management of the business goals and achievement of the business results driving the need for the program.

Benefits map provides traceability between project outcomes and deliverables to the benefits intended from the output of the program.

Benefits metrics allow for monitoring incremental benefits delivery; it should include incremental benefits delivery dates and quantifiable benefits delivery measures.

Benefits realization illustrates—and measures—precisely how projects and programs add true value to the enterprise.

Benefits realization plans formally document the activities necessary for achieving the program's planned benefits.

Benefits registers collect and list the planned benefits for the program and are used to measure and communicate the delivery of benefits throughout the duration of the program.

Business case is a document written for executive decision makers, assessing the present and future business value and risks related to a current investment opportunity.

Business-focused program management is a business-focused organization that is fully devoted and disciplined in its use of program management practices.

Business results are the tangible business outcomes that result from the creation and implementation of new products, services, and other capabilities delivered as the output of the programs.

Business value encompasses the synergistic improvements that program management can provide to optimize the business functions of the enterprise.

Budget hours variance is the difference between program budget and actual hours.

Budget resource variance is the difference between program budget and actual resources.

Budget variance is the difference between actual program costs and budget.

Bottom-up budget approach includes estimating component costs and consolidating them at the program level to calculate program budget.

Change control is a process whereby modifications to documents, deliverables, or baselines associated with the project are identified, documented, approved, or rejected.

Change control board (CCB) is a formally chartered group responsible for reviewing, evaluating, approving, delaying, or rejecting changes to the project, and for recording and communicating such decisions.

Change request is a formal proposal to modify any document, deliverable, or baseline.

Change request form is a document that outlines changes to the original program scope, time line, or funding, and provides justifications for them to help determine proper action.

Communication planning is an activity of determining the information and communication needs of the program stakeholders based on who needs what information, when they need it, how it will be given to them, and by whom.

Competitors rely on the benefits of the performing organization program as a component of one of their programs.

Component characterizes any part of the program, including subprogram, projects, and program operational management activities.

Critical path is the sequence of activities that represents the longest path through a project, which determines the shortest possible duration. See also critical path activity and critical path method.

Customers are individuals or organizations that will use the new capabilities/results of the program and derive the anticipated benefits.

Duration is the total number of work periods required to complete an activity or work breakdown structure component, expressed in hours, days, or weeks.

Enterprise resource is a part of the list of resources for the whole organization; therefore, each of these resources can be shared across multiple projects. Typically, the list of enterprise resources is managed by an administrator, and each project manager adds these resources to their projects as needed.

Environmental analysis is a process of identification of internal and external factors, analysis of their impact on the program, and development of a plan to mitigate risks that internal and external factors present to the program.

Facilitation-focused program management is a facilitation-focused organization that is also project-oriented, but the projects are normally grouped into programs organically rather than strategically.

Finish date is the last day when the task is executed. Finish date is frequently a scheduled finish date.

Forecast hours variance is the difference between program forecast and actual hours.

Forecast resource variance is the difference between program forecast and actual resources.

Forecast variance is the difference between program actual costs and forecast.

Funding organization is a part of an organization or an external organization providing funding for the program.

Gantt chart is a bar chart of schedule information where activities are listed on the vertical axis, dates are shown on the horizontal axis, and activity durations are shown as horizontal bars placed according to start and finish dates.

Gaps on the program management continuum represent a need for an organizational transformation from current to expected program management functions.

Generic resources are used to specify the staffing requirements for a project, such as carpenters and developers, or a team of resources.

Governmental regulatory agencies are organizations that operate within the regulatory and legal boundaries of their local and national sovereign governments, as well as other related nongovernmental organizations that set standards or requirements that are required to be adhered to.

High risk can significantly impact a program or a component cost, schedule, or performance.

Implementation checklist defines the steps required to implement the end state in this specific environment successfully.

Indicators show that the component management plans are linked to the program management plan.

Integration-focused program management function is an integration-focused organization that views projects as part of a program that is driven by the business strategy of the firm.

Low risk can minimally impact a program or a component cost, schedule, or performance.

Manually scheduled tasks have user-defined start, finish, and duration values. The project will never change the dates, but may warn you if there are potential issues with the entered values.

Matrix organization is defined as an organization where team members do not report directly to the program manager and are not solely focused on the program work.

Medium risk can somewhat impact a program or a component cost, schedule, or performance.

Microsoft Office Project Server is a project management server solution made by Microsoft. It uses Microsoft SharePoint as its foundation, and supports interface from either Microsoft Project as a client application or by web browser connecting to its Project Web App (PWA) component.

Microsoft Project is a project management software program, developed and sold by Microsoft, that is designed to assist a project manager in developing a plan, assigning resources to tasks, tracking progress, managing the budget, and analyzing workloads.

Monthly component actual cost is an amount of money that was spent to deliver component benefits in a given month.

Monthly component actual hours are calculated as a quotient between monthly component actual and resource hourly rates.

Monthly component actual resources are calculated as a quotient between monthly component actual hours and working hours in a month.

Monthly component budget is calculated as a quotient obtained by dividing the total component costs by component duration.

Monthly component budget hours are calculated as a quotient between monthly component budget and resource hourly rates.

Monthly component budget resources are calculated as a quotient between monthly component budget hours and working hours in a month.

Monthly component forecast cost is an amount of money that is forecasted to be spent to deliver component benefits in a given month.

Monthly component forecast hours are calculated as a quotient between monthly component forecast and resource hourly rates.

Monthly component forecast resources are calculated as a quotient between monthly component forecast resource and working hours in a month.

Non-enterprise resource, or local resource, is not a part of the list of resources for the whole organization. No other project manager can use your non-enterprise resources in their projects.

Organizational agility is the ability to change or adapt rapidly in response to market conditions or other external factors, including new competitors, emerging technologies, customer demands, and sudden economic and sociopolitical shifts.

Other groups are groups representing the consumer, environmental, or other interests.

Performing organization is a group that is performing the work of the program through component projects and non-project work.

Phase gate is a review at the end of a phase in which a decision is made to continue to the next phase, to continue with modification, or to end a project or program.

Point of transition represents a decision point where senior leaders make a determined choice to shift their organization from project-oriented to program-oriented.

Potential customers are past and future customers who will be watching intently to see how well the program delivers the stated benefits.

Predecessor activity is an activity that logically comes before a dependent activity on a schedule.

Program is a group of related projects, subprojects, and program activities managed in a coordinated way to obtain benefits not available from managing them individually.

Program actuals tracking process is a reoccurring process of obtaining actual program costs at the component level and for the program in total.

Program benefits delivery phase is a second and iterative phase of the program life cycle; during this phase a program manager plans, integrates, and manages the program components to facilitate delivery of the intended program benefits.

Program benefits management domain defines, creates, maximizes, delivers, and sustains the benefits provided by the program.

Program benefits management is a process of identifying program planned benefits and monitoring the program's ability to realize them.

Program benefits management strategy defines how a program will contribute to the realization of organizational strategic goals if the program receives necessary funds and is properly executed.

Program budget is total program costs that are required to deliver program benefits.

Program change control is a process whereby modifications to documents, deliverables, or baselines associated with the project are identified, documented, approved, or rejected.

Program closure phase is the third and last phase of the program life cycle; during this phase a program manager executes a controlled closure of the program.

Program definition phase is the first phase of the program life cycle; during this phase a program manager expands business case and strategic plan objectives and fully defines expected program outcomes.

Program earned value management is a program management technique for measuring program performance and progress in an objective manner.

Program financial framework defines program funding flow, ensuring that the money is spent efficiently.

Program financial management plan is a component of the program management plan that documents all of the program's financial aspects: funding schedules and milestones, initial budget, contract payments and schedules, financial reporting activities and mechanisms, and financial metrics.

Program forecast is a reoccurring process of estimating a program's future costs.

Program governance board members are responsible for authorizing and overseeing a program.

Program governance domain establishes processes and procedures for maintaining program management oversight and decision-making support for applicable policies and practices throughout the course of the program.

Program life cycle is a set of phases that are followed to deliver program benefits.

Program life cycle management domain manages all of the program activities related to program definition, program benefit delivery, and program closure.

Program management community of practice (PgMCoP) is a forum that allows program managers to influence business program management structure, sculpt business program manager roles, help standardize program management definitions and program domains, and share knowledge and best practices.

Program management continuum is an approach to program management within the organization structure that defines how organizations establish their program management functions.

Program management office is an organization responsible for defining and managing the program-related governance processes, procedures, templates, supporting individual program management teams by handling administrative functions centrally or providing dedicated assistance to the program manager.

Program management performance domains are complementary groupings of related areas of activity, concern, or function that uniquely characterize and differentiate the activities found in one performance domain from the others within the full scope of program management work.

Program management plan is a key document that guides a program manager and a program team through the program life cycle.

Program Management Professional (PgMP)® is a certification granted by PMI; it is a visible sign of your advanced experience and skill and gives you a distinct advantage in employment and promotion.[1]

---

[1] PMI (n.d.). Retrieved from http://www.pmi.org/en/Certification/Program-Management-Professional-PgMP.aspx

Program manager coordinates groups of related projects rather than managing individual projects.

Program operational management is a part of the program that includes elements of related work outside the scope of the discrete projects.

Program-oriented organizations are organizations that fully utilize program management, often viewing it as a part of the business management function and linking it to the corporate strategy.

Program planner is responsible for updating program plans and schedules (e.g., Gantt charts) to plan and subsequently report project progress. This role may exist in more complex programs.

Program procurement management addresses the activities necessary to acquire products and services.

Program risk is an event or series of events or conditions that, if they occur, may affect the success of the program.

Program risk management planning identifies how to approach and conduct risk management activities for a program by considering its components.

Program risk monitoring and control is the activity of identifying, analyzing, and planning for new risks; tracking identified risks and those on the watch list; and reanalyzing existing risks.

Program road map should be both a chronological representation in a graphical form of a program's intended direction as well as a set of documented success criteria for each of the chronological events.

The program sponsor is the individual responsible for championing the application of organizational resources to the program and for ensuring program success.

Program stakeholder engagement domain captures and understands stakeholder needs, desires, and expectations and analyzes the impact of the program on the stakeholders, gaining and maintaining stakeholder support, managing stakeholder communications, and mitigating stakeholder resistance.

Program steering committee is a committee that plays an important role in directing a program throughout program life cycle execution.

Program strategy alignment domain identifies opportunities and benefits to achieve the organization's strategic objectives through program implementation.

Program team members are responsible for various aspects of the program. They may contribute to the definition of the program's strategy or plan, or oversee and coordinate the activities conducted as part of the program's plan, including component and program operational management activities.

Program tools include a status report, risk tracking mechanism, and financial tools.

Project is a temporary endeavor undertaken to create a unique product, service, or result. The temporary nature of the project indicates that a project has a definite beginning and end.

Project critical path is the sequence of activities that represents the longest path through a project, which determines the shortest possible duration.

Project managers are change agents; they make project goals their own and use their skills and expertise to inspire a sense of shared purpose within the project team.

Project management office manager is responsible for defining and maintaining standards for project management within the program.

Project management software can help plan, organize, and manage resource tools and develop resource estimates.

Project Management Institute (PMI) is an international organization advancing the professional field of project management. It does this by setting standards, through certified education and development, and by conducting research and professional conferencing.

Project Management Professional (PMP)® is the most important industry-recognized certification for project managers granted by PMI.

Project management software can help plan, organize, and manage resource tools and develop resource estimates.

Project-oriented organizations are organizations that do not utilize program management to its full capacity and view the program management function only as an extension of the project execution that primarily realizes administrative needs.

Project planners are responsible for updating project plans and schedules (e.g., Gantt charts) to plan and subsequently report project progress. This role may exist in more complex projects.

Portfolio is a collection of projects, programs, subportfolios, and portfolio operational management activities grouped together to facilitate the effective management of work to meet strategic business objectives.

Quality management ensures that a quality plan exists for overall program and project quality.

Resources are typically people included in your project plan, whether or not they are assigned to tasks.

Resource-based approach to building a program management plan assigns resources to tasks, estimates hours of work based on task duration, and calculates program costs as a product of hours times resource rates.

Resource plan is a document that includes resource estimates and records all information about resources, including roles they will play in a program when they are on-boarded and off-boarded.

Resource planning is an activity of determining resource needs and timing when they are needed.

Resource prioritization allows the program manager to prioritize critical resources that are not available in abundance and to optimize their use across all components within the program.

Resource requirements is a document that outlines resource needs and defines the roles that resources will play in a program.

Return on investment (ROI) is the benefit to an investor resulting from an investment of some resource.

Risk is an uncertain event or condition that, if it occurs, has a positive or negative effect on one or more project objectives.

Risk manager is responsible for identifying potential risks in advance, analyzing them, and taking precautionary steps to reduce and mitigate risks.

Stakeholders represent all those who will interact with the program as well as those who will be affected by the implementation of the program.

Stakeholder engagement management is a process of communicating and working with stakeholders to meet their needs/expectations, address issues as they occur, and foster appropriate stakeholder engagement in project activities throughout the project life cycle.

Stakeholder engagement planning activity outlines how all program stakeholders will be engaged throughout the duration of the program.

Start date is the first day when the task execution will start. Start date is frequently a scheduled start date.

Statement of work (SOW) is a document that defines project-specific activities, deliverables, and time lines for a vendor providing services to the client.

Strategic plan consists of initiatives that are influenced in part by market dynamics, customer and partner requests, shareholders, government regulations, and competitor plans and actions.

Subprograms are programs that include individual projects and are managed as part of another program.

Suppliers are product and service providers who are often affected by changing policies and procedures.

System allows managing a program management plan and tracking program progress, assigning resources to tasks, analyzing workloads, and managing a budget.

Task mode shows if a task is scheduled manually or automatically.

Task name is the name of the task in the component or program. It is a text box that allows typing in any text, adjusting fonts, and applying formatting.

Task order number is the number in the leftmost column that lists task numbers in order starting with one.

Task percent complete shows partial or full completion of the task in percent values. Based on tasks percent complete, Microsoft Project and many other systems calculate components and program percent complete to date.

Time line is a way of displaying a list of events in chronological order, sometimes described as a project artifact.

The Standard for Program Management is the first document that provided a detailed understanding of program management, defined a standardized approach to it, and outlined methodologies to execute programs. PMI first published *The Standard for Program Management* in 2006. To date, PMI has published two subsequent editions.

Work breakdown structure (WBS) is a hierarchical decomposition of the total scope of work to be carried out by the project team to accomplish the project objectives and create the required deliverables.

References

Blomquist, T., & Müller, R. (2004). *Program and portfolio managers: Analysis of roles and responsibilities.* Proceedings of the PMI Research Conference (11–14 July), London, England.

Gardner, D. G. (2001). *Operational readiness—Is your system more "ready" than your environment?* Retrieved from https://www.pmi.org /learning/library/operational-readiness-system-ready-environment-7946

Karekar, H. (2014, April 14). *Escalation—Let's do it right!* Retrieved from https://www.projectmanagement.com/articles/283756/Escalation -Let-s-Do-it-Right

LaBrosse, M. (n. d.). *Email or phone conference? Making the most of communication technologies in each project phase.* Retrieved from https://www.pmiwdc.org/article/email-or-phone-conference- making-most-communication-technologies

Larson, R., & Larson, E. (2011). *Creating bulletproof business cases.* Minneapolis, MN: Watermark Learning.

Lovelace, J. (2016). *Interview.* MsPM, PMP, PgMP, Product Launch Management Advisor at Eli Lilly and Company.

Martinelli, R. J. (2016). *Interview.* Co-author of the book, *Program management for improved business results.* (2nd ed.). Hoboken, NJ: John Wiley & Sons, Inc., 2014.

Martinelli, R. J., Waddell, J. M., & Rahschulte, T. J. (2014). *Program management for improved business results.* (2nd ed.). Hoboken, NJ: John Wiley & Sons, Inc.

Martinelli, R. J., Waddell, J. M., & Rahschulte, T. J. (2014). Transitioning to program management. *PM World Journal, 3*(9), 1–3. Retrieved from http://pmworldlibrary.net/wp-content/uploads/2014/09/pmwj26-sep2014-Martinelli-Raschulte-Waddell-Introduction-to-Transitioning-to-program-management.pdf

Merrick, A. (2015). *Allied forces.* Retrieved from http://www.pmi.org/-/media/pmi/landing-pages/business-analysis-tools-silverpop/pdf/allied-forces-project-management-business-analysis.pdf

Project Management Institute. (2008). *The standard for program management* – Second edition. Newtown Square, PA: Author.

Project Management Institute. (2010). *What does it take to be a program manager? Established veterans advise up-and-coming project managers on how to make the jump program manager.* Newtown Square, PA: Author.

Project Management Institute. (2013). *A guide to the project management body of knowledge (PMBOK® guide)* – Fifth edition. Newtown Square, PA: Author.

Project Management Institute. (2013). *Pulse of the profession®: In-depth report—The high cost of low performance. The essential role of communications.* Retrieved from http://www.pmi.org/-/media/pmi/documents/public/pdf/learning/thought-leadership/pulse/the-essential-role-of-communications.pdf

Project Management Institute. (2013). *The standard for program management* – Third edition. Newtown Square, PA: Author.

Project Management Institute. (2013). *PMI's industry growth forecast: Project management between 2010 + 2020.* Retrieved from http://www.pmi.org/-/media/pmi/documents/public/pdf/business-solutions/project-management-skills-gap-report.pdf

Project Management Institute. (2014). *The project management office: Aligning strategy & implementation.* Retrieved from http://www.pmi.org/-/media/pmi/documents/public/pdf/white-papers/pmo-strategy-implement.pdf

Project Management Institute. (2015). *PMI—A global project management community.* Retrieved from https://www.pmi.org/membership/benefits/community

Project Management Institute. (2015). *PMI lexicon of project management terms, Version 3.0.* Newtown Square, PA: Author.

Project Management Institute. (2015). *Pulse of the profession®: Capturing the value of project management through organizational agility.* Retrieved from http://www.pmi.org/-/media/pmi/documents/public/pdf/learning/thought-leadership/pulse/capture-value-organizational-agility.pdf

Project Management Institute. (2016). *Pulse of the profession®: The high cost of low performance—How will you improve business results?* Retrieved from http://www.pmi.org/-/media/pmi/documents/public/pdf/learning/thought-leadership/pulse/pulse-of-the-profession-2016.pdf

Project Management Institute. (n.d.). *Who are project managers?* Retrieved from https://www.pmi.org/about/learn-about-pmi/who-are-project-managers

Ramani, S. (2016). *Interview.* Director, GRT Consulting LLP

Stuckenbruck, L. C. (1979, September). The matrix organization. *Project Management Quarterly.* Retrieved from https://www.pmi.org/learning/library/matrix-organization-structure-reason-evolution-1837

About the Author

Irene Didinsky, MBA, PMP

Early in her career, Irene Didinsky recognized that project and program management was her passion. She accepted roles of increasing complexity and responsibility in a broad range of industries, including healthcare, energy, utilities, food and beverages, power tools, and hospitality. Ms. Didinsky led global cross-cultural projects at Deloitte. She delivered programs that implemented value-based care solutions for large healthcare systems at Evolent Health, a healthcare consulting firm. And, she has influenced the delivery of millions of dollars of capital investment through project and program management at Kaiser Permanente.

As there are very few books written about program management, Ms. Didinsky became a writer by night, while working as a program manager. Her enthusiasm for helping people in all aspects of program management flows through in the expert program management knowledge that she has shared in this book. Successful collaboration with the Project Management Institute (PMI) added tremendous value to the book. The book's content fully attests to *The Standard for Program Management* published by PMI.

She holds a bachelor of science degree in engineering from the Ural State Polytechnic University in Russia, and an MBA from the University of Chicago Booth School of Management. She obtained her Project Management Professional (PMP)® certification in 2008, and she joined PMI that same year.